BISHOP BART PIERCE

COVER ME
IN THE
DAY OF BATTLE

BISHOP BART PIERCE

COVER ME
IN THE
DAY OF BATTLE

THE SIGNIFICANCE OF
SPIRITUAL FATHERHOOD
FOR THIS GENERATION

STRAWBRIDGE
press

PUBLISHED BY STRAWBRIDGE PRESS
1607 Cromwell Bridge Road, Baltimore, MD 21234
Phone: 410-882-2217 Website: www.rockcitychurch.com

Unless otherwise identified, Scripture quotations in this book are taken from **NKJV** New King James Version. Copyright © 1982 by Thomas Nelson, Inc. Used by permission. All rights reserved.

The following abbreviations are used to identify other versions of the Bible in this book:
KJV *King James Version,* also known as the *Authorized Version.*
The Message *The Message, The Bible in Contemporary Language*, by Eugene H. Peterson. Scripture quotes from *The Message* Copyright © 1993, 1994, 1995, 1996, 2000, 2001, 2002. Used by permission of NavPress Publishing Group. All rights reserved.

Nouns and pronouns referring to deity are capitalized throughout the text of this book unless they are included within a direct quotation, in which case the original capitalization is retained.

Includes bibliographical references.
ISBN: 0-9776892-1-2

Edited by Cynthia Ellenwood, Signature Editions, Atlanta, Georgia
www.signature-editions.net

Cover design by Ed and Mary Ann Edman, ED&M Design
www.edmdesign.net

Printed in the United States of America.
First Printing March 2006

Read what these leaders are saying about
Cover Me In The Day Of Battle

Do you desire to be or believe you are a spiritual warrior? Then this book is for you! You need to read this prophetic proclamation and explanation of what every "spiritual warrior" (spiritual son, daughter, mother or father) needs and must have. *Cover Me In The Day of Battle* is a timely, revelational, anointed book. Bishop/Apostle Bart Pierce has written a bold and prophetic tour de force. Get ready for a fascinating read from someone who, like Jesus, has authority with vulnerability. The hardest thing you will experience in reading *Cover Me In The Day Of Battle* is that you won't want to stop reading once you start. A discourse resource and must read.

APOSTLE JOHN KELLY
Founder and overseeing apostle
Antioch Churches and Ministries

Bishop Bart Pierce has blessed us with his book, *Cover Me In The Day Of Battle*, which is the exciting story of sons and fathers. One statement is worth the price of the book: "Our goal is not finding the perfect father, nor finding perfect people to follow us. Our goal is to receive the Father's blessing wherever we are, under the covering where God has placed us, and to be fathers." Bart's revelation on coats having the significance of authority and blessing is powerful. You will be most interested in reading about the three coats in Joseph's life. And about why he says some local churches have failed to be anointed and blessed because they have become harlots. Don't miss that one. Finally, we learn why many young ministers are happy with brothers but not fathers. He has done a great favor for the Body of Christ in this book. I think it is the best thing he has ever written, and not just because he put my name in the book.

PASTOR CHARLES GREEN
President, Harvest Ministries To The World
Founding Pastor of Faith Church, New Orleans, Louisiana

"Who is your daddy?" is the question often raised in a competitive challenge; but in the world of the kingdom it has become a catchphrase. "Who is your Father?" This question is often asked by those seeking to add to their "stables of pastors" persons who are desperately in need of mentors and legitimate spiritual fathers. Bishop Pierce's penetrating study is born out of a consistent, walk of accountability with proven men of God, and he understands the need of the novice and the mature to walk in genuine accountability.

This book can be a manual for those who are looking for a model and for those who are seeking affirmation for what they have come to believe is an essential idea for those without any kind of authority structure.

BISHOP JOSEPH L. GARLINGTON, SR.
Senior Pastor of Covenant Church of Pittsburgh
Presiding Bishop
Reconciliation! Ministries International: A Network Of Churches and Ministries

CONTENTS

SECTION III. ENTERING THE WORLD OF FATHERING

*"For the earnest expectation of the creation
eagerly waits for the revealing of the sons of God."*

*"Now, therefore, you are no longer strangers and foreigners, but
fellow citizens with the saints and members of the household of
God, having been built on the foundation of the apostles and
prophets, Jesus Christ Himself being the chief cornerstone."*

*"And he said to him, "Every man at the beginning sets out the
good wine, and when the guests have well drunk, then the inferior.
You have kept the good wine until now!"*

SECTION I.

BLESSINGS OF SONSHIP

INTRODUCTION

"O GOD the Lord, the strength of my salvation,
You have covered my head in the day of battle." [1]

I find it interesting to consider how a book like this comes into creation. This has been the result of years of personal experiences, messages I've preached, and people I've seen shipwrecked on the journey, and longed to help.

When I began to write this book I was led to Psalm 140. The title "Cover Me In The Day Of Battle" comes from David's cry to God in Psalm 140:7.

The message of covering is found throughout the Word of God. Adam was covered by God, His Father, yet he turned away from Him and His loving, caring protection and chose to cover himself with some leaves. Although there was life in the leaves (oxygen), it was a counterfeit covering, and man has been making up ways to cover himself ever since.

God often refers to Himself as our Covering, and He has provided many other coverings for us, just as a mother hen covers her young chicks. The blood of Jesus cleanses us and covers our sins. Parents cover us. Worship and praise cover us as we come before God.

When I became a Christian in 1972, I began a whole new journey of understanding about my life and the need for covering. I saw how uncovered I had become before I was

---

[1] Psalm 140:7.

saved, and therefore how vulnerable I had been to Satan, life's circumstances, and especially the consequences of my own actions. My parents (one of God's great coverings) had died some time earlier, and I had become naked to every trick of the enemy and every desire of my flesh. When I became a new believer, I found peace and safety. I knew that God was my Covering forever, and because I was saved in a church, I also found myself under the wonderful covering of my pastor. I now had someone whom I could trust and bounce things off of pertaining to the issues I was dealing with in my life. I was also confronted with my need to cover my wife and our new baby who was on the way.

It was awesome to have a pastor who loved me and prayed for me. After all those years without any kind of covering in my life, things began to really come together. I learned how to pray and received counsel from my pastor, which created a great sense of safety. Proverbs says there's great safety in a multitude of counselors.[2] Over and over again, God's counsel helped me to line up to the place where I should be and where I am today—in the center of God's will for my life.

I marvel at how many people make the strange statement that they don't need a covering. Some argue that abuse could come when some man is covering you. While there will always be those who take the truth and pervert it or twist it for their own gain, because I had a personal prayer life and I was in God's Word for myself, my pastor's counsel was a blessing. It was another witness to me that I was hearing God clearly. It was not the only witness, but his counsel confirmed what I heard God saying to me.

One day while I was preaching about Elisha and Elijah, suddenly I saw their story in a whole new light. When Elisha asked the prophet Elijah to give him a double portion of his anointing, I saw that it meant something entirely different from what I had understood before. I had preached and heard preached many great messages about the double portion that

---

[2] See Proverbs 11:14.

Elisha wanted—greater anointing, greater miracles, greater power than Elijah had before him. Granted, after Elijah left Elisha did twice as many miracles as Elijah had done, but it wasn't just some transferred gifting that he wanted or received. He wanted a spiritual father, and he received the rights of that double portion that the eldest son receives as his inheritance from his father.[3] I began to understand what Jesus meant about those who would come after Him when he said, "Greater works than these shall you do in my name." [4]

Anointing flows down from the head to the feet.[5] The power is greater at the bottom of the flow, like the increased force of a waterfall when it hits the ground, or like the anointing at the hem of Jesus' garment that was touched by the woman with the issue of blood.[6] We have authority when we are at the bottom—when we are under authority. Those who aren't under authority have only their own authority or what they can get from their religion, which is man-made fig leaves. When the fig tree didn't produce any fruit, Jesus cursed it. [7]

All authority comes from God and is transferred through a father to a son.[8] Many are learning to be fathers in this day, and transferring authority to their sons. We discuss that in several of the chapters.

It is important to be a father, but it is equally important to be a son first. God's greatest desire and the groan of the world is for mature sons.[9] You become a mature son by growing up under a father. Remember, when God started this whole thing He started it with a son—Adam—not a baby or an old man.

Life is full of battles every day. David knew the importance of having his head covered, especially in the day of battle. Goliath's downfall came because the giant did not

---

[3] See Deuteronomy 21:17.
[4] See John 14:12.
[5] Psalm 133:2.
[6] See Matthew 9:20.
[7] See Matthew 21:19.
[8] See Matthew 28:18.
[9] See Romans 8:22.

have his forehead covered. David knew God had sent him to defeat Goliath. He declared, "I've come in the name of the Lord." [10] He was covered by his father, Jesse, who had sent him to the battle, and he was covered by his early mentor, Saul, who covered him and told him to go fight for Israel. David knew that his head was covered in the day of battle.

Is it possible that so many good soldiers—intercessors, pastors, leaders, sons—are cut short in the time of their greatest potential because they've gone to battle without their heads covered? In the day of do-it-yourselfism, isn't it time to get honest with ourselves and those under our care and stop trying to be politically correct about the subject of submission and discipleship? Isn't it time to address the need for sonship as we face these real issues at hand?

Remember, submission means coming under the mission of another. Sure, there are dictators and tyrants in the world and in the church, but that doesn't mean that we should throw away the truths in the Word of God that say we are to be submitted to one other. Jesus said, "Take care of another man's field and you'll have your own one day." [11]

Fathers, arise now, and raise up sons. Sons, arise, and get your heads covered, and let's go to battle. As you read this book, my desire is that the curse of fatherlessness will be broken, and sons will turn to fathers and fathers will turn to sons, [12] so that the Church can be the force God created it to be. The Church can stop the epidemic of fatherlessness by once again becoming the light of the world—providing a true example of fatherhood that displays the picture of what great relationships between true fathers and sons look like. Enjoy.

---

[10] See 1 Samuel 17:45.
[11] See Luke 16:12.
[12] See Malachi 4:6.

CHAPTER 1

HOPE FOR THE FATHERLESS

". . . thou art the helper of the fatherless." [13]

Fatherlessness is at the root of almost every social battle we face today. If I asked the people in most churches how many were raised without a father, chances are that more than half of them would raise their hands. Absentee dads neglect their children. We call them deadbeat dads. Many women end up raising children alone.

What is the cry of people all over the world? They want fathers. What is destroying the inner city? The lack of fathers. Through the pain of the world, God is prophesying to the Church that the Church needs to change.

In the Bible, God used natural disasters to speak to Israel. First the natural, then the spiritual. [14] The Church has tried to turn it around and blame the world for fatherlessness, but it isn't the world's fault that this is a fatherless generation. It's the Church's fault. Society is reflecting a problem in the Church.

Many people come to church with an unfulfilled

---

[13] Psalm 10:14 KJV.
[14] See 1 Corinthians 15:46.

longing for a father, but because of their life experiences they may actually reject the kind of father they need. How great is the task of the spiritual father, when the son or daughter has no example on which to base that much needed relationship?

This generation is troubled, but I have great hope for this generation because of God, "the Helper of the fatherless."[15] In fact, I would go so far as to say that this will be a "Miracle Generation." We are in a battle, but through embracing spiritual fatherhood, people alive today will change America and the nations of the world. I don't know all of them yet, but I am looking for them. They are the ones who know their need for a father's covering in the day of battle, just as God, our Father, covers us.

| Cover me in the day of battle | "O GOD the Lord, the strength of my salvation, You have covered my head in the day of battle." [16] |

Fatherhood, the solution for fatherlessness

Fatherhood is one of the most powerful forces in the earth, and God is about to release a wave of fatherhood through the Church. He is doing something much bigger than what you and I might see in just a few people's lives. He is doing something much broader than the people we submit to or the people we disciple. God is shaking nations. He is putting down some governments and setting others up.[17]

> *This book is a call to spiritual fatherhood, and it is also a call to sonship—the willingness to submit your life to a father, so that you can receive the father's blessing.*

God has authority that He is ready to release to the Church in this hour of shaking. I believe that He will release it

---

[15] Psalm 10:14 KJV.
[16] Psalm 140:7.
[17] Psalm 75:7 KJV.

to those who are not afraid of commitment. They are not afraid to change their lifestyle to serve a man of God. They are empowered by the biblical obedience of sons and daughters honoring their father.[18]

> *We have a choice today. We can either cooperate with God's covering of spiritual order and protection from those in authority over us, or we can rebel against it. I have chosen to cooperate with the covering that God has placed in my life. This gives me strength for the daily battles of life—for myself and those whom God has given me.*

Pastor Charles Green and I have had a relationship and friendship for more than 30 years. He provides an apostolic covering over my life and ministry. I am a pastor, and provide a pastoral covering for many people, yet I myself have covering as well.

We have many coverings in our lives that God has given us for our protection and growth. There's the covering of a father and mother.[19] There's the covering of marriage.[20] There's the covering of friends.[21] There's the covering of government.[22] There's the covering of ministry and pastoral oversight.[23] There's a covering of authority in our lives at every dimension and at every level.

Mary understood Jesus' covering of her life
Jesus' mother showed that she understood covering and God-ordained order at the wedding in Cana when she said to the servants, "Whatever He says to you, do it."[24] She wasn't sure

---

[18] See Exodus 20:12.
[19] See Ephesians 6:1-3.
[20] See Ephesians 5:21-33.
[21] See John 15:13-14.
[22] See Romans 13:1-7.
[23] See 1 Corinthians 4:14-21.
[24] John 2:5.

if Jesus was going to do anything, because He said His time had not yet come, but she said, "Whatever this Man tells you, just do it!"

Mary said, "Whatever He says to you, do it."

"On the third day there was a wedding in Cana of Galilee, and the mother of Jesus was there. Now both Jesus and His disciples were invited to the wedding. And when they ran out of wine, the mother of Jesus said to Him, 'They have no wine.' Jesus said to her, 'Woman, what does your concern have to do with Me? My hour has not yet come.' His mother said to the servants, 'Whatever He says to you, do it.' " [25]

In this case the Son was the covering for His mother. She knew that Jesus would know what to do, and He would need people in place to do it. Then God would move.

Apostolic covering of the early Church

We will never get to the place where America is shaken by revival until all of us, as Christians, lose our independent spirit and follow the spiritual leaders whom God has given us.

Just as the 11 apostles took time in the upper room to replace Judas and fulfill the bishopric before the outpouring of the Holy Spirit came at Pentecost,[26] the good things that we would like to see in our generation will come to pass as men rise up to fulfill their duty as fathers. Then we will see an outpouring on sons and daughters who are changed by their fathers' blessings.

---

[25] John 2:1-5.
[26] See Acts 1:20-26.

This ministry of apostleship

"And they prayed and said, 'You, O Lord, who know the hearts of all, show which of these two You have chosen to take part in this ministry and apostleship from which Judas by transgression fell, that he might go to his own place.' And they cast their lots, and the lot fell on Matthias.

"And he was numbered with the eleven apostles." [27]

POWER OF A FATHER'S BLESSING

Jacob cheated to get his father's blessing,[28] and he paid for it later in life. Yet what Jacob desired was a good thing. He desired the blessing of his father. Esau was hungrier for soup than for his birthright, but Jacob wanted his father's blessing.

A father's blessing is more powerful than the will of man. It is more powerful than the imperfections of a father or child. It is more powerful than the spirit of fatherlessness. A true father with God-ordained authority who speaks a blessing over his children can shape the rest of their lives for good.

I can't tell you how many people would give their right arm for one sincere blessing from their fathers. Real sons value the blessing of a father—not his money, his fame, or his coattails. If you want to get close to a man of God to try to get a title, an open door to preach, or a financial blessing, you are going after the soup of Esau. If you are going down and going after the presence of God in his life, then you want the blessing.

Elisha wanted his spiritual father Elijah's blessing. Some people come to church on Sunday to get a little more head knowledge, but they haven't a clue what God is saying.

They are like the students in the school of the prophets

---

[27] Acts 1:24-26.
[28] See Genesis 25:29-34; 27:1-29.

9

who said to Elisha, "Guess what? We know some juicy stuff! Elijah is going to leave!"

Elisha said, "Guys, I know that, just be quiet." They kept their distance, but he stayed close to his father Elijah so that he could get his mantle. He wanted something that they didn't want. He wanted a father.

Students go after Elisha

"And it came to pass, when the Lord was about to take up Elijah into heaven by a whirlwind, that Elijah went with Elisha from Gilgal. Then Elijah said to Elisha, 'Stay here, please, for the Lord has sent me on to Bethel.' But Elisha said, 'As the Lord lives, and as your soul lives, I will not leave you!' So they went down to Bethel. Now the sons of the prophets who were at Bethel came out to Elisha, and said to him, 'Do you know that the Lord will take away your master from over you today?' And he said, 'Yes, I know; keep silent!' " [29]

WHY YOU SHOULD LOVE BEING A SON

You will overcome fatherlessness in your life when you stop *wanting* to be fatherless. Why would anyone want to be fatherless? Because you don't understand the benefits of a father's covering. You want to stay in charge. You love independence more than you love the father's blessing.

When you love being a son, you welcome opportunities to show respect and submit to a father on earth. Through your experiences with your father, you learn how to become a great father yourself. You no longer want to stay

[29] 2 Kings 2:1-3.

young and irresponsible. You want to grow up and be a dad, just like your dad.

The blessings of sonship occur in both the natural and the spiritual realms. They occur in natural father and son relationships, and also in spiritual father and son relationships. Ultimately, they begin with your relationship with your Father in Heaven. Just as He is our covering in the day of battle, earthly fathers are a covering for their natural and spiritual sons as they deal with the personal battles everyone faces in their daily lives.

WHY SONS RESIST SONSHIP

Spiritual orphans by choice

What happens when people want to have a father but have no desire for sonship? They become "independent," but not in a good way. We think of being independent as being self-sufficient and strong, but that is not what I am talking about. I am talking about people who are so rebelliously independent that they become disconnected from covenant relationships. They become self-reliant, self-promoting, self-protecting, and self-centered. They are spiritual orphans.

Spiritual orphans bounce from church to church like regular orphans do in the foster care system, trying to find someone in leadership to focus on them the way they focus on themselves. Let's face it, you will never find a church that is in love with your ego as much as you are!

These people are not always the ones who come across as emotionally strong. Some of the most weepy, seemingly "dependent" people are fiercely self-centered and disconnected. They are needy, but their needs are never met because they don't know how to function in a family environment. They set their own agenda. They show up when they want to show up. They don't follow the leadership in the house.

No experience in resolving family conflicts

Have you ever met someone who was an only child, or who has only one child? They think that homes are supposed to be quiet, and everything is supposed to be clean and orderly all the time. They see two kids tussling and they don't know what's going on. People from normal families understand that conflict, fights, and offenses happen in family life. They understand that in a family, you give up some of your rights. You don't get to be first all the time. You don't get to have what you want for dinner every single night. You have to wait for the shower sometimes, and there's no hot water left.

No heart for sonship

Spiritual fathering is lacking in society and the Church because so few have a heart for sonship and submission.

- They don't understand the benefits.
- They want to stay in charge.
- They are unwilling to become sons, so they don't bring out the fatherhood in others.
- Instead of opening their hearts to love and respect their dads, they close their hearts and judge them. When they find their fathers imperfect, they reject them.
- They want the father's inheritance without paying the price of sonship.
- They want to maintain their lives as independent rebels, so they perpetuate the spirit of fatherlessness.

> *Our goal is not finding the perfect father, nor finding perfect people to follow us.*
> *Our goal is to receive the Father's blessing wherever we are, under the covering where God has placed us, and to be fathers.*

If I stood at the front of a church and called for all the perfect fathers to rush to the altar for everyone to see, do you

12

think I would get a huge stampede? Yet just as imperfect fathers in the natural still provide the stability and protection that is needed by their children, incomplete spiritual fathers can do their job in your life while they are still learning and growing. You can safely submit to an imperfect father—spiritual or natural—when you keep your eyes on your Heavenly Father, Who placed you under him.

My personal history of rebellion
Everyone starts out as a rebel in one way or another. My story is no exception. I lost my mom at the age of 9. I started doing drugs at the age of 13. I threatened to beat up a teacher who was failing me, and ended up with a B. The school wrote a letter promising to mail me my diploma if I would stay away from graduation!

I made it through life by rebelling. By the time I got saved at the age of 22, I had more than 40 felonies, multiple arrests, and jail time to my credit. There couldn't have been a more rebellious hardhead than me.

God did something wonderful in my life and gave me a father through my willingness to submit. His fatherhood was not brought to the surface in my life until I decided to be a son.

Once I was saved, I immediately realized that I had to submit, and not just to an invisible God. I had to submit to an earthly man. I had no idea how to do that, so I just went to my pastor and listened. I told him that I knew nothing about Christianity—not one verse in the Bible. I had worked construction and had run heavy equipment for years, so I brought my nail bag and tools and offered to serve him in any way I could. He smiled and told me to do this, and I did it. He told me to do that, and I did it. Before I knew it, God was changing me.

What happened as a result? If I can say anything about my life so far, I can say that I went on to become a good father. I became a good father because I had become a good son. God gave me sons when I became one. So when I tell you that God helps the fatherless by causing them to desire sonship, I know what I am talking about.

GOOD SONS MAKE GOOD FATHERS

When Christians submit themselves to sonship, they will learn how to become fathers. Being a good son is the only thing you have any control over in this process anyway. I have people in my church who were just like me. They came from a dysfunctional background. God saved and healed them, and they found a connected set of relationships in our church. They found that they were able to submit to God to an even greater degree when they submitted to a father in the church. They became immersed in the vision and plan of God through sonship, and now they are becoming fathers with sons and daughters of their own.

EMPOWERED BY A FATHER'S COVERING

Joseph, who came from a family of 12 sons, had the favor of his father. Jacob gave Joseph a garment that was hand-woven of many different colors. It covered him completely, yet he had to grow to fill it out. Joseph was the one who shaped the garment as he grew. It was given to him, yet it was shaped by his unique features.

Circumstances in Joseph's life would force many different garments on him, yet he never forgot what it was like to have on that special garment from his father. Through prison, slavery, and eventually prosperity, all he really desired was that garment of favor from his father.

When you clothe your children as a spiritual father, circumstances in life can't erase the impact. Not every father affirms the calling of his son as Jacob did. Some see sons as a threat to their authority. Some are like jealous older brothers, and not spiritual fathers. When they see that you have favor on your life, it provokes them to "one-up" you with an exaggerated testimony, rather than joining you to rejoice.

> *Israel loved Joseph more than all his children, and he made him a coat.*

"Now Jacob dwelt in the land where his father was a stranger, in the land of Canaan. This is the history of Jacob. Joseph, being seventeen years old, was feeding the flock with his brothers. And the lad was with the sons of Bilhah and the sons of Zilpah, his father's wives; and Joseph brought a bad report of them to his father. Now Israel loved Joseph more than all his children, because he was the son of his old age. Also he made him a tunic of many colors. But when his brothers saw that their father loved him more than all his brothers, they hated him and could not speak peaceably to him. Now Joseph had a dream, and he told it to his brothers; and they hated him even more." [30]

  I learned from Pastor Green that a true spiritual father will always rejoice with you over the favor of God in your life. He can listen to me talk for hours about what God is doing, and will laugh and rejoice with me. That blesses me.

  Joseph may have been young and naïve, but he responded to the favor of his father by faithfully enduring trials. Some people receive the smallest amount of favor and become arrogant. They get blessed with the tiniest check, one little speaking engagement, or a healed toe, and they forget almost immediately that it was the grace of God. The next thing you know they're writing a dissertation on their own qualifications, and what you can do to be like them. They prove immediately that they can't be used as a spiritual father to transfer blessings to the next generation.

---

[30] Genesis 37:1-5.

OBEDIENCE BLOWS OUR MINDS WITH BLESSINGS

The Church today doesn't realize that through simple obedience, God will blow our minds with blessings. People are enjoying the wine of the spirit that has been poured out, and they should. Yet they don't realize that if they can obey whatever Jesus says, something even bigger, even greater, will be poured out. The relationships of spiritual fathering work in concert with what God is doing overall.

This may be the most awesome and exciting time to be alive. We are watching pivotal transitions in the Body of Christ. We are watching colorless water changed into the wine of a powerful spiritual outpouring. Yet some will miss it. Some will be in church for exactly the same amount of time as others, and miss it all.

Are you willing to do whatever Jesus tells you, like His mother?

Do you desire your father's blessing enough to go after it, like Jacob?

Do you want to get close enough to see it, like Elisha?

Will you wear your father's garment through the battles of life, like Joseph?

Something's about to happen. Can something happen in you?

CHAPTER 2

POWER OF A FATHER'S BLESSING

*"And he shall turn the heart of the fathers to the children,
and the heart of the children to their fathers. . . ."* [31]

O ne of the first things that people say after they give their hearts to the Lord Jesus Christ is that they want to go and reconcile with their fathers. Their father may have been wrong most of his life, but with the help of the Holy Spirit they instinctively know it is *their* responsibility to make peace. They want their father's favor.

> *I've sat at the hospital beds of dying men when
> the last light in their eyes is fading away, and
> their final words to me were, "Oh, how I'd love
> to feel the embrace of my father."
> Grown men crying out to once again
> feel the strength of a father!*

When sons and daughters get it in their hearts to start looking for their fathers, they will call everyone they know, search the Internet, check phone books and the Yellow Pages,

---

[31] Malachi 4:6 KJV.

scour the countryside, check police stations and hospitals, and even fly around the world, trying to find their fathers.

Fatherhood speaks to us of blessing. There is something comforting and empowering about being loved by your father. Recall how the Old Testament ends with the promise that in the last days God will send the spirit of Elijah "and he shall turn the heart of the fathers to the children, and the heart of the children to their fathers." [32] We need this heart for one another across the generational boundaries, because God says that the opposite of that father-child relationship is a curse. [33]

God's solution for the curse of fatherlessness	*"And he shall turn the heart of the fathers to the children, and the heart of the children to their fathers, lest I come and smite the earth with a curse."* [34]

The blessing that comes when hearts of fathers and children are turned toward one another speaks not only of the relationships of natural fathers and natural children. It also speaks of relationships between spiritual fathers and spiritual sons—sons who are backslidden and away from God coming back to the house of God and saying, "I've had what Egypt can give me. I've worn the finery of Egypt, but my father's humble coat is what I want."

Father's garment of blessing

Recall how Joseph, as a young man, brought a bad report to his father about his brothers. He told his dad they were lazy and not producing what they should. A brother who does that isn't going to win a popularity contest, but he had a standard inside that he lived by.

We know that Israel [Jacob] loved Joseph more than all of his children. Joseph was a son of his old age, the son of his first love, Rachel. He was born late in Jacob's life, and he

---

[32] Malachi 4:6 KJV.
[33] See Malachi 4:6.
[34] Malachi 4:6 KJV.

was such a favorite of Jacob that the father blessed his son with a special tunic, a coat of many colors. I can imagine it as brilliantly colored, a beautiful garment with threads of many hues running through it. When his brothers saw what their father had done, they said, "Look, Dad loves him more than he loves us." They hated him and couldn't speak peaceably to him.

The favor of God always provokes the jealousy of man. Favor attracts jealousy. It's going to happen. People do not want you to succeed. Joseph's brothers conspired against him, and made him their prisoner, then they sold him into slavery. They felt the coat of their father's favor as they ripped it from his shoulders. Naked and screaming, Joseph was carted off into slavery. Then his brothers covered the stain of their sin with the blood of a goat, clothing themselves in garments of deception.

In the days ahead, Joseph would wear other coats, but he would never lose the love of his father's covering that he had felt in that coat. It shielded him from the dishonorableness of Potiphar's wife who tried to seduce him.

Joseph remained a man of deep convictions. He remembered his father's garment.

"And it came to pass after these things that his master's wife cast longing eyes on Joseph, and she said, 'Lie with me.' But he refused and said to his master's wife, 'Look, my master does not know what is with me in the house, and he has committed all that he has to my hand. There is no one greater in this house than I, nor has he kept back anything from me but you, because you are his wife. How then can I do this great wickedness, and sin against God?' " [35]

Finally, when Joseph had to run from the seducing wife of Potiphar, he left his Egyptian coat behind. He was

---

[35] Genesis 39:7-9.

running as a moral young man. His convictions were still working strongly in him as he ran out of Potiphar's house.

When this woman accused him falsely, another garment was put on him when he was thrown in prison, yet still the covering of his father's love kept him. His integrity didn't leave him. He was a model of righteousness, the son of a patriarch, speaking into the lives of those in prison with him.

> *When you've felt a father's love and you realize*
> *what it means to be under a spiritual covering*
> *and live in right relationship with your father,*
> *you can go down into the pits of prison—even*
> *to the pits of your thought-life, and never*
> *become a prisoner.*
> *That's what a father can do.*

Do you know that Joseph didn't have those prophetic dreams that angered his brothers until after he got the coat? We know that his brothers didn't like him because of the favor of their father, and so of course they hated his dreams of future mastery over them. We have thought they hated him because of what he said, but it was because of what he was wearing.

In later years, after Joseph was released from prison and given favor with Pharaoh, can't you see Joseph standing on a rooftop watching for his dad to appear? I can see him clutching his royal Egyptian garment. He's rubbing the inlaid jewels that have been sewn into it and turning its golden linen threads. He looks nervously out over the desert, because this is a day that he has prayed for a thousand times.

He's wearing the finest robe that Pharaoh could provide, but he remembers another garment that he was given long ago—a coat of many colors, a coat of favor from his father. Joseph would have traded the finest robe of Egypt to wear that coat once again.

Remember, his father had the coat. The brothers had given it to him deceptively with the stains of an animal's blood, and all these years Jacob had thought that he was dead. I've often wondered if his dad got the little coat cleaned and brought it to his son. In my imagination I could see Israel coming along, leaning on a staff (because he's had a meeting with an angel and he's still limping). Joseph picks him out of all of the 75 people with him—the older man who won't let anybody help him. On the little donkey behind him somewhere, tucked up inside, is the little coat folded so nicely for his long-lost son.

GARMENTS OF THE FATHER'S ANOINTING

We know that Israel and Joseph were reunited, and the theme of fatherhood continues to fill the Scriptures. About 400 years after those scenes took place, the people of Israel had become slaves, and the Bible says, "Now there arose up a new king over Egypt, which knew not Joseph." [36] God remembered His covenant, and over a period of the next few years He raised up the Israelite child Moses, once again in the household of a Pharaoh, to become a deliverer.

God chose Moses' brother Aaron as priest, and gave him holy garments to wear. At the same time, God ordained that Aaron's garments would be passed down to his sons. These holy garments would carry the favor of God, the favor of their father, and the anointing of their father's priesthood.

Father's anointed garments to be passed to his sons	*"And the holy garments of Aaron shall be his sons' after him, to be anointed therein, and to be consecrated in them. And that son that is priest in his stead shall put them on seven days, when he cometh into the tabernacle of the congregation to minister in the holy place." [37]*

These holy garments were literally soaked in anointing oil. They were passed down from father to son, still soaked in

---

[36] Exodus 1:8 KJV.
[37] Exodus 29:29-30 KJV.

21

oil. With each generation, the anointing would increase and the fragrance would be enriched.

> *These garments of anointing represent something about a father's holiness and consecration that needs to be restored to the body of Christ. Those garments were so different from other types of clothing that are being passed off as legitimate by the Church today. The garments of anointing carry the favor of God, our Father, or a father's anointing. The new ones are often imitation garments.*

Imitation garments

I see two types of imitation garments being worn in the Church today:

- Fig leaves
- Uniforms

Fig leaves were the first man Adam's fleshly attempt at covering up his sin life. Fig leaves are cheap and uncomfortable. For those sitting in the pews, fig leaves can keep you looking OK on Sunday, but not OK before God.

Fig leaves don't wear well for a pastor. He may start out looking fine, but in a few years he's not pastoring any more because he's had an affair. The serpent came along and seduced him. He's not serving God any more, but he's still trying to make money: selling the tapes, selling the books, keeping the TV show going.

Someone recently told me what happened after he preached against pornography on a popular Christian TV station. He was pulled aside and told he would never be invited to preach there again. He was talking about righteousness, but someone in charge didn't like it because he was leading a double life.

Uniforms are given out by some church associations instead of a father's garment. They're made in a store and they all look alike. Winkin', Blinkin', and Nod. When you don't have fathering in the church, you have managers and administrators. All they know to do is fit you in an artificial coat that looks like everybody else's coat. It's never seen the Shekinah glory. When you put it on you think you're now anointed because you're in the blankety-blank denomination. You think you can walk in that. You say, "I went to Bible School. I studied hard," but when you lay hands on people, nothing happens. You stop praying, but you have learned some church growth tricks and you know how to cover the next generation with clothes that were made at a factory, and to give them the principles that you read somewhere. Uniforms are an artificial covering, just like fig leaves. They wear out because there is no anointing. They stifle growth and personal devotion to Christ. Instead of bringing healing to the generation, they make people sick.

Garments of the father's anointing and healing
God wanted careful preparation made for the garments that He would use to clothe Aaron—garments to pass down to his sons. God was building something into those garments that would last generationally. God honored and endorsed fatherhood in the priestly ministry from the start.

Preparation of garments of the father's anointing	*"And thou shalt speak unto all that are wise hearted, whom I have filled with the spirit of wisdom, that they may make Aaron's garments to consecrate him, that he may minister unto me in the priest's office."* [38]

Garments of the father's anointing. Aaron, the father, received garments, grew into them, soaked them in the anointing, then passed them down to his sons.

---

[38] Exodus 28:3 KJV.

23

In the Kingdom of God, sons and daughters build on what their fathers have accomplished, then take it to the next level. An earthly kingdom wouldn't last long if there were no generational transfer within a royal family. In the same way, the Kingdom of God should be building the future on the anointing of the last generation.

If you clothe yourself rebelliously without the covering of a father, your carnal attempts to appear dignified and sinless will not stand the test of time. You will have no understanding of how to clothe your children. The next generation, if there is one, will be unable to function in their gifts and callings because they, too, are wearing fig leaves and uniforms. Fading fig leaves and a color-by-numbers uniform can't hold the oil of the anointing.

We wonder why so many young ministers and youth pastors are falling and becoming tragic casualties in the war to expand the Kingdom of God. We don't recognize that we're sending them off in fig leaves and uniforms, not garments of favor.

We're putting them through a cookie-cutter Bible school or training program, not handing them garments backed by generations of godliness. We are not equipping these young upstarts with what they need to cover them. Unless God intervenes supernaturally, they fall.

Garments of the Father's healing. When you carry an anointing for which you and your father have paid a price, someone your garment touches can be healed from years of plague. Jesus spoke openly of His desire to please His Father. He said that His effectiveness in ministering to people was a direct result of His desire to please His Father: "I do nothing of myself; but as my Father hath taught me, I speak these things. And he that sent me is with me: the Father hath not left me alone; for I do always those things that please him." [39]

Do you consciously desire to always please your heavenly Father? Do you reach for the hem of his garment?

Healed by touching Jesus' garment

"A woman who had suffered a condition of hemorrhaging for twelve years—a long succession of physicians had treated her, and treated her badly, taking all her money and leaving her worse off than before—had heard about Jesus. She slipped in from behind and touched his robe. She was thinking to herself, 'If I can put a finger on his robe, I can get well' The moment she did it, the flow of blood dried up. She could feel the change and knew her plague was over and done with.

"At the same moment, Jesus felt energy discharging from him. He turned around to the crowd and asked, 'Who touched my robe?' . . .

"Jesus said to her, 'Daughter, you took a risk of faith, and now you're healed and whole. Live well, live blessed! Be healed of your plague.' " [40]

The anointing in Jesus' garment healed a woman He called "daughter." This woman had been bleeding for years. Her own capacity for normal, healthy intimacy had been destroyed. She certainly could not have borne children. Yet when she just touched Jesus' garment, she was healed.

---

[39] John 8:28-29 KJV.
[40] See Mark 5:25-34.

Allowing Yourself To Get Close To Someone

Do you wear a garment that carries an anointing?

Where did you get it?

If you have one, is it something that you could pass on to your sons?

Have you allowed yourself to get close enough to a spiritual father for him to clothe you with his favor?

Have you risked the displeasure of your brothers for the greater pleasure of being a son?

Have you been so willing to submit to the correction of your father that it became his pleasure to clothe you?

Have you provoked your father with your zeal to follow in his steps?

God wants us not only to submit to the coverings that He has set in place, but also to desire them. I believe that the next chapter on "Understanding Coverings" will make what I have said up to this point begin to fall in place for you, and you will want what God wants for your life at a new level of desire.

CHAPTER 3

UNDERSTANDING COVERINGS

". . . submitting to one another in the fear of God." [41]

A few years ago, The Southern Baptist Convention updated "The Baptist Faith and Message" to include the statement that a husband is to cover and protect his wife. More about what happened to them as a result of that statement in a minute.

Covering is a legitimate biblical concept of layers of protection and love over us, beginning with God. God covers my head in the day of battle.[42] I cover and watch out for my wife, and I am also covered by someone—a ministry leader who serves as my spiritual father, Pastor Charles Green.

We are in the midst of a war for truth, and we need to cover one another now more than ever. Covering protects my head from being deceived in the spiritual battles of life and keeps me encouraged that I'm on the right track.

Satan is shooting straight at my head. I wear my salvation helmet,[43] but Jesus said it is possible that even the

---

[41] Ephesians 5:21.
[42] See Psalm 140:7.
[43] See Ephesians 6:17.

elect can be deceived and seduced in their minds.[44] I don't want to face the wrath of God[45] because of something stupid the devil puts in my mind, so I keep my head covered. Pastor Green is my spiritual father. That doesn't mean that he pays my salary or orders me around. I don't owe allegiance to him because of a paycheck. I voluntarily submit my life to him because I understand the benefit of God's protection and order that is expressed to me through his covering.

People who provide covering in human relationships offer leadership and guidance. They give counsel and perspective. They help insulate you from the criticism, discouragement, and mixed signals of the world. But only if you let them.

The Baptist statement on husbands and wives concluded with this sentence: "A wife is to submit herself graciously to the servant leadership of her husband even as the church willingly submits to the headship of Christ." [46] All of a sudden, all hell broke loose because the Baptists had said that they believed what the Bible said. You know, there's a lot of stuff in this Bible that's not going to make you happy. You better get hold of that truth real soon.

Listen to me. I've been at this too long to be playing games with you. I am dead serious—straight as an arrow. I don't mind saying what needs to be said. Too many church people are floating all over creation and they're uncovered. They're running around exposing themselves. Their nakedness is a shame to the kingdom of God. God is telling us in this hour to get covered.

I want to say this to you as plainly as I can. *God wants to cover you.* He wants to cover every aspect of your life. He wants to cover you with Himself and He wants to cover you

---

[44] See Mark 13:22.
[45] See Ephesians 5:6.
[46] *The Baptist Faith and Message 2000.* Online at http://www.sbc.net/bfm/bfm2000.asp.

with people like your natural and spiritual father, and if you're a wife, He wants you to be covered by your husband, just as Christ covers the Church.

> *We're living in a day of battle when people don't want to hear the truth. They would rather hear a lie. Even in the Church, people refuse to believe the Bible. They would rather believe what fits their own little flesh.*

Saints, you need the covering of the Word. It will set you free. It will change your life. It will convict you. If you're out of line it will make you miserable, but it will heal and change you. Covering is such a practical provision from the Creator, it must be amazing to Him how much we wrestle with something that is that simple. It reminds me of when I traveled to Japan and the bed was too short and the blanket didn't reach my feet. Even when I curled up at night, my feet stuck out. Covering is great. It's cold when you are uncovered.

This debate about covering is about who's ruling the nation, who's ruling the world, who's in charge. This is about Satan and God. This is about whose kingdom and whose dominion.

Covered by a husband

When the Bible says a wife submits herself to her husband, it doesn't mean he can take out a rod and a whip and a chain. It doesn't mean that her husband can become some kind of dictator. In fact, the Bible says to submit yourselves one to another in the fear of God.[47]

| *A husband covers his wife* | *"For the husband is head of the wife, as also Christ is head of the church; and He is the Savior of the body."* [48] |

When the Bible talks about marriage in Ephesians 5, it

---

[47] See Ephesians 5:21.
[48] Ephesians 5:23.

is actually speaking about Christ and the Church. Jesus is our covering, and the Bible says that His love for us is like a husband's love for his wife. His covering is like a husband's covering.

> *Husbands cover their wives as Christ covers the Church. They are the hinges on the door of the home. Whatever comes in and goes out is up to them. They are aggressive against anything that would hurt the family under their protection.*

COVERING IS GOD'S IDEA

Covering is not some Baptist's idea. It is not even the Church's idea. It's God's idea. It's a good idea. It's all over the Bible.

The Lord covers us all day long | *"The beloved of the Lord shall dwell in safety by him; and the Lord shall cover him all the day long, and he shall dwell between his shoulders."* [49]

I want to dwell in the safety of the Lord. Don't you? I don't have to be independent from God to be happy. I'm not running *from* God. I'm running *to* God. I say to Him, "Cover me, God!" I want His covering, and if He sends some human being to cover me, according to His best plan for my life and my ministry, I'm not running from that, either. I'm going to get under.

The Bible describes many different coverings, in addition to a husband's covering of his wife.

God covered Adam and Eve after they sinned.[50]

God covers us with destiny in our mother's womb.[51]

---

[49] Deuteronomy 33:12 KJV.
[50] See Genesis 3:21.

30

He covers us with the oil of anointing.[52]
He covered Israel with the cloud of His presence.[53]
He covered the mercy seat of the Ark.[54]
He covered the Tabernacle in the wilderness to protect the holy things of God from the desert sun and dust storms.[55]
He said to cover the nakedness of the priests.[56]
He covers our worship with His glory.[57]

God covers us with His cloud of glory when we worship Him

". . . indeed it came to pass, when the trumpeters and singers were as one, to make one sound to be heard in praising and thanking the LORD, and when they lifted up their voice with the trumpets and cymbals and instruments of music, and praised the LORD, saying:

> *'For He is good,*
> *For His mercy endures forever,'*

that the house, the house of the LORD, was filled with a cloud, so that the priests could not continue ministering because of the cloud; for the glory of the LORD filled the house of God." [58]

He covers us with His blood.[59]

Covered by His blood
When the children of Israel were about to be released from

---

[51] See Psalms 139:13.
[52] See Psalms 133:1-2.
[53] See Psalms 105:39.
[54] See Exodus 25:20.
[55] See Exodus 26:7.
[56] Exodus 28:42-43.
[57] 2 Chronicles 5:12-14.
[58] 2 Chronicles 5:12-14.
[59] See Revelation 7:14.

slavery in Egypt, God told them to cover their doorposts with the blood of a lamb, so that the plague of the death angel would not strike their houses.[60] When Jesus died for us, He covered our sins with His blood and made us right with God, and now we walk in fellowship with one another.

Jesus' blood cleanses and covers us	*"But if we walk in the light as He is in the light, we have fellowship with one another, and the blood of Jesus Christ His Son cleanses us from all sin." [61]*

When the devil sees our garments of salvation,[62] he stops short and says, "Hold it! That person is off limits!" Thank God for His blood covering of salvation.

Covered with Jesus' life
When Jesus covers you, He covers you with life. He covers you with glory. He covers you with healing. He covers you with deliverance. He covers you with joy. He covers you with every good thing that's in the Bible. He covers you with mercy. He covers you with truth. He covers you with grace. He covers you when you're naked. He covers you when you're clothed. He covers you when you're ugly. He covers you when you're pretty. For the ladies, He covers your eyes when you love some ugly guy and can't see how ugly he is.

Covered by church government
Sometimes in ignorance people find themselves in situations where they are uncovered. They are naked to the elements of the world, Satan, demonic activity, and all manner of harassment from the dark world. That's why we need the Church. Churches are cities of refuge that provide covering in a time of crisis. When Rock City Church established a home for women who were without a covering, we called it "The Hiding Place." The church is their covering.

---

[60] See Exodus 12.
[61] 1 John 1:7.
[62] See Isaiah 61:10.

The Bible lays out a governmental structure of leaders in the fivefold ministry. We are to respect those who cover us.

Respect those who watch out for your soul	*"Obey those who rule over you, and be submissive, for they watch out for your souls, as those who must give account. Let them do so with joy and not with grief, for that would be unprofitable for you."* [63]

JESUS HAD AUTHORITY WITH VULNERABILITY

Whatever is not producing vulnerability to God in your life is keeping you deceived that you are in charge, when you're not. Jesus demonstrated vulnerability when He stripped Himself to wash the disciples' feet on the night He was betrayed.[64] He was ridding Himself of an earthly covering to make a point about a higher purpose. He gave us the perfect picture of laying aside human coverings to show that He was under the covering of His Father and the will of God.

Jesus taught by His example that having authority doesn't mean we dominate people. We don't set ourselves up to be above anybody else by claiming they need our covering. We serve them from a position of lowliness. We're not too good to do the dirty work it takes to serve others. I unclog my own toilet. I blow my own nose. I bleed real red blood like everyone else. I'm always looking at what I can take off, not what I can put on. I'm not trying to place any more layers between myself and the people I am fathering. I'm not putting on anything artificial for the benefit of getting their respect.

WHEN YOUR HEAD IS UNCOVERED

When David had to kill Goliath, he aimed for the most

---

[63] Hebrews 13:17.
[64] See John 13:4.

33

vulnerable spot—his head. Unless you cover your head, as mentioned earlier, your mind is open to the missiles of the enemy. He wants to shoot you in the head, so keep it covered. When you reject your covering, one of the first things that happens is that your thinking becomes distorted. You get confused. You can pray and read the Bible all night, but you're still confused about God's will for your life.

> *If your life is in disarray, maybe it's because you're uncovered. You need to submit yourself once again to that husband or pastor who was covering you. Don't analyze and nitpick about that relationship. Covering is too important. Let God clean up the details.*

If you are uncovered because of your rebellion, or because you are outside of the church or have departed from your faith, you are vulnerable to seducing spirits.[65] Those spirits will try to suck you into deception and pull you away from the truth of God. Don't let them.

Numbers 19:15 says that "every open vessel, which has no cover fastened on it, is unclean." A container that is physically uncovered gets dirty. It is subject to the elements of the world. The same is true of people who are uncovered— they become exposed to the harsh and destructive forces of the world, and often they become contaminated.

Counterfeit coverings ("fig leaves")
Sometimes people create their own imitation coverings when they don't like the coverings that God has given them, as I said in Chapter 2. Adam and Eve sewed fig leaves together for a covering in Genesis 3. Can you imagine walking around in homemade underwear put together from leaves and twigs? It's not any different today when people cover themselves with fame, power, intellectualism, and other forms of temporary success. Does that impress God?

---

[65] See 1 Timothy 4:1.

We settle for counterfeit coverings for the same reasons that we should pursue real coverings—the need for protection and order. The devil's counterfeit coverings come packaged with worry, guilt, fear, and doubt. We need to strip ourselves of false coverings and go back under the coverings of God.

False religious coverings (uniforms)
Some people put on a false religious spirit to cover their lack of consecration. They say "Hallelujah! Praise the Lord!" but they don't tithe. They put on a form of godliness but have no real power to protect themselves, and they live with the burden of keeping up appearances.

When the Apostle Paul discovered that Peter was covering himself with a false religious legalism left over from Judaism, he confronted him, because this false covering was hindering the expansion of the Kingdom. Even apostles need other apostles to cover their backs.

I ministered once to a young woman from a background where she thought she had to cover herself with long skirts, long hair, and no make-up. Now I don't think you have to wear make-up to be beautiful, but her "holiness" was giving her a sour expression. She grew up as a Christian, but she was obsessed with protecting her virtue by controlling her outward appearance. She was hindered from worshiping God in church services because she was so conscious of the makeup and jewelry of other women. When faced with a former prostitute who needed ministry, she was paralyzed because she couldn't embrace her in that flimsy clothing.

Eventually, she came to me for prayer because she had to go in for major surgery. I asked her if the doctors would take off her clothes for the procedure. "Of course," she answered. I asked her if she really believed God could show up for her surgery if she were in a scanty hospital gown. That may seem silly to you, but it opened her eyes! She asked me to pray for her deliverance, and finally she was free!

DESIRE FOR GOD'S COVERINGS

I know that I'm going to stay covered. I want the coverings of God over me. I don't want to be a rebel. I don't want to be a do-my-own-thing Christian.

You know, I could go anywhere. I could preach anywhere. I could do anything I want to do, but I know that I need to continue to stay covered. That's where the joy is, the life, the love, the power. That's where I find peace and hope. It's my protection. God's coverings put me in a place where I can stand and say, *"Na-na na-na na-na!"* to the devil and he can't touch me!

They overcame the accuser by the blood of the Lamb	*". . . the accuser of our brethren, who accused them before our God day and night, has been cast down. And they overcame him by the blood of the Lamb and by the word of their testimony, and they did not love their lives to the death."* [66]

That's right. I'm bought and paid for by the blood of the Lamb. My responsibility is to live out this life before God through all the day-to-day challenges that test my commitment, and to stay faithful.

Don't you want the coverings over your life that God has prepared for you with His infinite wisdom?

If you don't have a spiritual father speaking into your life, wouldn't you like to know how to find one?

Whether or not you have a spiritual father yet, it will help you to learn more about how you can be a great spiritual son. Then when it happens, you will be ready, and when you become a father, you will know what to expect in your son.

---

[66] Revelation 12:10-11.

SECTION II.

RESPONSIBILITIES
OF SONSHIP

CHAPTER 4

BECOMING A GREAT
SPIRITUAL SON

". . . as the firstborn by giving him a double portion of all that he has, for he is the beginning of his strength; the right of the firstborn is his." [67]

There is a group of people in the Church today who are rising above the mediocre. They carry themselves like sons. They hang around the man of God. They show up whenever he calls a meeting. Maybe they began by humbly carrying his bags or driving him to a speaking engagement, but now they are carrying his anointing.

Just as a natural son resembles his father, these spiritual sons resemble the best character qualities of the man of God who is over them. They bring the same fire to their preaching. They have the same results in their ability to reach people. They become just as dedicated and consecrated as the man who is their leader and their covering in the church.

---

[67] Deuteronomy 21:17.

Another group of people might be in the same church but they act like those students in Elisha's day who kept their distance from Elijah. They come and listen, but they never quite understand what the preacher is saying to them about the power and purpose of God. They just sit in church—when they decide to come—and they may even ask some questions, or create some turmoil, but they go home unchanged. They are not becoming sons.

How does someone become a great spiritual son? What are the benefits? What are the sacrifices required?

GOING AFTER A MAN OF GOD

Sons who go after a spiritual father's mantle and his anointing are like Elisha, who focused his attention on Elijah's every move when most of those around him were distracted by incidentals. A lot of people hung around Elijah, and probably most of the sons of the prophets had at one time or another thought about getting Elijah's mantle, but Elisha was the one who got it. Why? Elisha was different. The others were students; Elisha was a son. A son is the one who receives the inheritance. In fact, according to the Bible, the firstborn son receives a double portion.[68] That's what Elisha went after—a double portion.[69]

Elisha was a businessman. He went after Elijah with the same zeal as a person closing a business deal, but for a higher purpose. Once he saw that the man of God was approachable and had something from God, he couldn't rest until he found exactly what it would take to reach him and receive that anointing. As Jesus said about the disciples who were following Him, when you go after a man of God, you can do what He does and even greater things.

---

[68] Deuteronomy 21:17.
[69] See 2 Kings 2:9.

| *Sons can do greater things than their fathers before them* | *"The person who trusts me will not only do what I'm doing but even greater things, because I, on my way to the Father, am giving you the same work to do that I've been doing. You can count on it."* [70] |

That's what ended up happening with Elisha, and that's what can happen to you. Whom are you going after with the mindset that you will become greater than he is?

CULTIVATING A FATHER'S FAVOR

Elisha had several factors in his favor that you need to cultivate so that you can go after a man of God, become his son, and begin to do those greater things that a son does.

- Servanthood
- Sensitivity to sonship
- Obedience
- Independence from insensitive people
- Closeness
- Watchfulness

The Church will progress at a greater pace when each generation builds on the one before, and exceeds it in obeying God's Word.

If this is the Miracle Generation, as I believe it is, not only technology will increase exponentially every year, but also the Church and the level of fathering that takes place there.

Let's look at each of the qualities of sonship that will help you to become a better son, or if you are already a son, to increase even more in your anointing.

---

[70] John 14:12 *The Message.*

41

Servanthood

Elisha was a businessman when Elijah showed up one day and
threw his mantle over him, but he immediately became a
servant. A tremendous honor had been bestowed upon him,
but his response wasn't to exalt himself. His response was to
humble himself. He leaped into action.

Elisha's call to servanthood	*"So [Elijah] departed from there, and found Elisha the son of Shaphat, who was plowing with twelve yoke of oxen before him, and he was with the twelfth. Then Elijah passed by him and threw his mantle on him. And he left the oxen and ran after Elijah, and said, 'Please let me kiss my father and my mother, and then I will follow you.'*
	"And he said to him, 'Go back again, for what have I done to you?'
	"So Elisha turned back from him, and took a yoke of oxen and slaughtered them and boiled their flesh, using the oxen's equipment, and gave it to the people, and they ate. Then he arose and followed Elijah, and became his servant." [71]

Elisha didn't mind doing something messy for the sake
of the man of God. He took his oxen and killed them, then
took time to prepare and serve them to the people around him.
He blessed the people with whom he was working. He blessed
them without expecting anything in return.

A lot of church-going student types are not like Elisha.
They think that their knowledge exempts them from heavy
lifting. They don't want to be servants. They want to come in,
get a message and become a prophet. They don't want to go
through the process of letting God do something with them, if

---

[71] 1 Kings 19:19-21.

they would only become a servant. Elisha didn't hesitate. He didn't pause or struggle inside. He had a heart to serve.

Sensitivity to sonship

Elisha was sensitive to sonship. He wanted his father's *impartation*, not just his *information*. Elisha saw himself as a son at the feet of his father, covered by the father's mantle. While the students in the school of the prophets were waiting for the next sermon, Elisha was waiting for the mantle. While the students were pressing him for the latest news tidbits, Elisha was unimpressed, and told them, "Shut up!"

Those students in Elijah's day were like people who come to church to hear a new message from their favorite preacher, but they don't come when he's away. They are not sensitive to his spirit. They ignore his pleas to come to church in his absence, because, like any good father, he has provided a good meal for them even if he can't be there.

Students are not like sons. They take notes that fill up their Bibles, then never look at them again. Six months down the road they drop the Bible and leaflets fly everywhere. They pick them up and say, "Well, I'll be, I haven't seen this. . . . I forgot. . . . Oh, look at this!" What are you taking the notes for? "Ever learning, and never able to come to the knowledge of the truth." [72]

Elisha's sensitivity to sonship

"And so it was, when they had crossed over, that Elijah said to Elisha, 'Ask! What may I do for you, before I am taken away from you?' Elisha said, 'Please let a double portion of your spirit be upon me.' So he said, 'You have asked a hard thing. Nevertheless, if you see me when I am taken from you, it shall be so for you; but if not, it shall not be so.' " [73]

[72] 2 Timothy 3:7 KJV.
[73] 2 Kings 2:9-10.

43

A son values the impartation because he sees the man of God as a father, not just a teacher giving talking points. As a son, he sees his relationship with the man whom God has placed over him as something permanent. Just like a natural father-son relationship, he sees that this thing is for life.

A double portion of a father's inheritance went to the firstborn son, according to Deuteronomy 21. When Elisha asked for a double portion of the spirit that was on Elijah, he was not asking for a monetary inheritance or even the supernatural ability to do the things Elijah did. He was already wealthy, and he was already anointed. Elisha was asking to be a spiritual son by asking for the inheritance that is due a spiritual son. We might think of the passing of the mantle and the double portion to Elisha in terms of spiritual feelings. We might think of tingles and goose bumps and fire coming out of our hands and eyes. But Elisha was asking for sonship.

Obedience

The first time that Elijah gave instructions to Elisha, he obeyed. He was being prepared to be an obedient son.

Elisha demonstrated obedience	*"And [Elijah] said to him, 'Go back again, for what have I done to you?' So Elisha turned back from him."* [74]

Jesus is my perfect model of the obedient Son. By His obedience, the Bible says, "many will be made righteous." [75] I must consider, then, how my obedience to those over me can allow me to have a greater impact on those under me. As I honor my father, I honor God and my life and ministry are blessed.

When I was saved, I knew that I should be an obedient son to the man who led me to the Lord. It wasn't up to me to judge him, just to follow him. I made sure I didn't have a spirit of suspicion, just a spirit of discernment. My discernment was

---

[74] 1 Kings 19:20-21.
[75] Romans 5:19.

focused on the will of God for my life, not on dissecting the inner workings of my pastor's brain.

Honor your father and mother, and it will be well with you	*"Children, obey your parents in the Lord, for this is right. 'Honor your father and mother,' which is the first commandment with promise: 'that it may be well with you and you may live long on the earth.' "* [76]

Independence from insensitive people

When the students talked to Elisha they said, "Guess what? We know some juicy stuff! Elijah is going to leave!"

Elisha said, "Guys, I know that, just be quiet. You guys are a bunch of morons."

Elisha knew that he was about ready to get something valuable from his father. He wanted something that they didn't want, and all their silly dialogue could easily get him off track. He wasn't influenced by the pressure of his peers.

Closeness

The sons of the prophets wanted to be around Elijah, but they never poured water on his hands. Elisha gave the prophet a drink and he got a prophet's reward. You can't throw someone a drink from 14 feet away. You have to be close. When you are close to a prophet you inevitably expose your weaknesses and flaws and receive correction. That is why most church people keep their distance. They are afraid of something they need from a father—correction.

It's hard for people to accept rebuke, so they stay away from those with a higher standard than theirs. Some people figure if they get a little close, but not too close, some of the good stuff will just fall on them and they won't have to get committed. So they hang out at church and are close enough to see the move of God, but they never jump in the water.

Have you ever met somebody who keeps his distance? He is right in front of you, but you can tell there's a

---

[76] Ephesians 6:1-3.

disconnect. Maybe he looks down; or you shake his hand, and he is looking at someone else. People like that want the mantle of the prophet, just like Elisha, but they don't want the commitment that comes with closeness. They want the anointing, the demonstration, and the gifts, but they want to do it at a distance. They are checking it out, and talking about it, but they are afraid to surrender to it.

God is not giving them the mantle. Maybe they were in the church the same amount of time as everybody else, but they missed the visitation because they took a break and then He came. They were not there to catch the mantle when God showed up because they did not have enough closeness to be sensitive to their spiritual father.

Watchfulness
Unless you watch your father's signals and learn his ways for a long time, you can't predict where he's going, and be there.

Elisha kept watching Elijah	*"When the LORD was about to take Elijah up to heaven in a whirlwind, Elijah and Elisha were traveling from Gilgal. And Elijah said to Elisha, 'Stay here, for the LORD has told me to go to Bethel.' But Elisha replied, 'As surely as the LORD lives and you yourself live, I will never leave you!' So they went on together to Bethel."* [77]

The life of a man of God is unpredictable. He can't be constrained by the needs of those around him. He has to respond to the Spirit. Therefore, a spiritual son is always watching his father for signs. He can't predict everything his father will do, because his father is not accountable to him, so he makes himself accountable to his father. He doesn't serve his father at his own *convenience*. He serves the father at his *inconvenience*. That takes watchfulness. The Bible says that

---

[77] 2 Kings 2:1-2 NLT.

Elisha wouldn't leave Elijah even when told to go away. You might call it righteous disobedience. While everybody else just talked, Elijah waited and watched.

Lots of people would love to flow in the gifts of a man of God, but few are willing to watch him to see how he cultivates those gifts in his prayer life and daily devotion, day in and day out. Watching someone who teaches you something with his life is different from learning bits of information from someone in the pulpit. It forces you to absorb much more subtle aspects of that person's character. Those who want quick answers from the top will never have the patience to watch. And it goes without saying that as a spiritual father to others, your life must be worth watching.

Elisha saw what he had been watching for

> "... *suddenly a chariot of fire appeared with horses of fire, and separated the two of them; and Elijah went up by a whirlwind into heaven.*
> *"And Elisha saw it."* [78]

The students didn't know exactly when Elijah's departure was going to happen, but incredibly they didn't bother to stay close. They had more pressing business. As a result, they missed the moment that they were looking for. If they had known, they would have been there when the chariot showed up, but the Bible says that they were way off. Elisha was watchful. He wouldn't let Elijah out of his sight, even though Elijah tried to send him away. Sons living with their fathers are watching them all the time. They live with them until they come of full age. They become like their fathers from hanging around them.

There's something about the way God works that requires watchfulness. Jesus rebuked His disciples for their lack of it, and down through the centuries He will be rebuking us, if we're not careful. In the Garden of Gethsemane He said to Peter, James, and John, "What! Could you not watch with

---

[78] 2 Kings 2:11-12.

Me one hour? Watch and pray, lest you enter into temptation. The spirit indeed is willing, but the flesh is weak." [79]

REWARDS FOR SONS ARE WAITING

Sonship is costly, and sometimes even godly fathers can't find sons willing to pay the price. If you read all of the story of Elijah in the Bible, you'll see that he had already been through seven cities before he produced a spiritual son.

It's hard for a father to find spiritual sons today, but if you initiate a relationship with a spiritual father, and work on that relationship, some spiritual father is going to get blessed.

Sometimes the things that are the most costly also bring the greatest rewards. If you decide you will no longer look at church as a place where you are a sometime student, getting a bunch of knowledge and then going home, you can become something else—a son who says, "I want more." Every time your "Elijah" says, "Go home," you can say, "Nope! I ain't goin'!" Then you will be a son. You will know how to be disobedient, in righteousness.

Think generationally—sons submitting to fathers and sons raising up sons, anticipating that each generation will exceed us. Remember, Jesus said, "He who receives a prophet in the name of a prophet shall receive a prophet's reward." [80] Rewards await you. They are just around the corner. Keep running. When you get thirsty from running, where can you get living water to refresh you so that you can keep on running? You need wells. Let me tell you where the wells are. If they are stopped up, I can help you fix the problem with those wells so that you can get down to where the water is.

---

[79] Matthew 26:40-41.
[80] Matthew 10:41.

CHAPTER 5

FINDING THE FATHER'S WELLS

"He that believeth on me, as the scripture hath said,
out of his belly shall flow rivers of living water." [81]

I n the midst of a famine, the Bible says that Isaac went
looking for the wells of his father. He had been blessed by
God with many flocks and multiple resources, just like his
father Abraham before him, but without fresh water he could
have lost it all. In his need, he looked for his father's wells.

When Isaac found his father's wells, he discovered that
his father's enemies, the Philistines, had spitefully filled the
wells with dirt. Isaac had to dig out the dirt to find water for
his family and his flocks.

> ***Isaac dug again his father's wells***

"And Isaac dug again the wells of water which they had dug in the days of Abraham his father, for the Philistines had stopped them up after the death of Abraham. He called them by the names which his father had called them." [82]

---

[81] John 7:38 KJV.
[82] Genesis 26:18.

We have a similar problem today. In order to find the spiritual wellsprings of our fathers, we have to dig through the dirt that enemies have stuffed into our fathers' wells. The world, the flesh, and the devil discredit fatherhood and deny that the wisdom of fathers is something worth digging for in this generation.

Wells for drinking water
Water is still the number one issue faced by nations today. Everyone needs water—clean drinking water. We can't live without it. In every natural disaster, from a tsunami to a Category 5 hurricane, one of the first considerations is getting clean drinking water to the people. In the same way, countless people are thirsting spiritually, desperate for God's living water to survive. We expect to get water whenever we turn on the faucet, but in reality we need the wells of our fathers to take us through the droughts of life.

Wells for cities
In the time of the patriarchs, whole cities were built around wells. They were the source of life for people and their flocks. A good well could last a thousand years and provide refreshing for generation after generation. We know that Jesus met the Samaritan woman at Jacob's well,[83] which was still providing water long after he had died. Even in times of drought or in the desert, a well can keep producing water to keep people and livestock alive.

Wells of salvation
Wells help us understand the greatness of our salvation. Isaiah said, "Therefore with joy you will draw water from the wells of salvation." [84] When you find yourself in a rough place, you take a big ladle full of water from the wells of salvation and drink, and you can laugh at your enemy. You dip in your cup and find joy, because of Jesus. You can do all things with joy.

---

[83] See John 4:6.
[84] Isaiah 12:3.

Instead of going from problem to problem, you go from glory to glory.[85]

Wells full of dirt

Wells are life-sustaining when water is flowing, but useless when full of dirt. When the Bible says that the wells of Isaac's father Abraham were full of dirt, it says to me that they were full of man, who is made of the dust of the earth. The wells were full of the wrong stuff. The right stuff couldn't come out because of the dirt.

Abraham left an inheritance for Isaac, but it was not all clean. Abraham also passed along some of his weaknesses, like Isaac's recent escapade just before he went looking for his father's wells. Isaac, like his father, had become fearful and lied to a king about his relationship with his wife, and allowed her to be taken into the king's harem.[86]

> *However, just because Isaac had to dig out the*
> *dirt in his father's wells doesn't mean that*
> *there wasn't any water there under all the dirt.*
> *The water was worth digging for. Don't give up*
> *on your father's wells, just get past the dirt to*
> *the water. It's in there somewhere for you*
> *because you're a son of your father.*

Finding enough wells for all

The water was worth fighting for, because every time Isaac dug out a well and found water, enemies came back to strive with him. He had to keep looking for another well, and then he had to dig the dirt out of that one, too. Finally, the Bible says, he found a well where his enemies stopped striving with him.

---

[85] See 2 Corinthians 3:18.
[86] See Genesis 26:7.

| *Finding a well that no one quarreled over* | *"And he moved from there and dug another well, and they did not quarrel over it. So he called its name Rehoboth, because he said, 'For now the Lord has made room for us, and we shall be fruitful in the land.' "* [87] |

BUILDING THE FAMILY NAME FROM WITHIN

Job, said, "Is not my help in me?" [88] All of us who have Christ have a well within us,[89] so the picture of wells could apply to the Church generally, but I want you to see the picture from your personal point of view. Look at your own heart for a minute. What is in your well? If you had a son and the son came looking for water from his father, would he first have to deal with some dirt inside of you that is stopping up your well when he needs water?

| *Rivers of water overflowing with life, if you believe in Jesus* | *"On the last day, that great day of the feast, Jesus stood and cried out, saying, 'If anyone thirsts, let him come to Me and drink. He who believes in Me, as the Scripture has said, out of his heart will flow rivers of living water.' But this He spoke concerning the Spirit, whom those believing in Him would receive; for the Holy Spirit was not yet given, because Jesus was not yet glorified."* [90] |

The Bible says that Jesus came to destroy the works of the devil.[91] We have learned to bind him, resist him, reject him, and all those other things, but we haven't been dealing

---

[87] Genesis 26:22.
[88] Job 6:13 KJV.
[89] John 7:38 KJV.
[90] John 7:37-39.
[91] See 1 John 3:8.

enough with destroying the devil and his works of dirt and darkness. You have dark places in you that are like the inside of a well. There is water inside, but there is also dirt to be removed. Some of the devil's dirty work may be going on in you, just as it is everywhere else in the culture, if you're not careful, but you can defeat him.

Jesus said that if you believe in Him, out of your belly shall flow rivers of living water.[92] Are you flowing with living water? If you're not flowing, or if you want a greater flow, you can unstop your well by digging out the dirt. If there's no flow of living water from wells that you have inherited from God and from your spiritual and natural fathers, get out your shovel and dig. You can unstop those wells.

The word "son" in Scripture means a builder of the family name. It means a builder of nations. God told Abraham that his seed (his sons, his ancestors) would be multiplied like the grains of sand.[93] Isaac was a son, a builder of the family name of Abraham. Isaac's son Jacob (Israel) was a builder of the family name of Abraham, Isaac, and Jacob. We still reference them today, thousands of years later.

> *How do you build your family name? You build*
> *on the foundation of those who have gone*
> *before you by going back to find what they have*
> *left to you as a spiritual inheritance.*

Sometimes you may have to dig past the dirt, but you can still honor them and make the family name great because of what they have left you that endures through the generations. Some families never achieve glory because no son cared enough to remove the dirt. Still other sons respond to the dirt they see by kicking in more!

When your family line honors God and gives Him His proper place, every generation increases not only the fame of the family name but also the fame of the name of God. God's

---

[92] See John 7:38.
[93] See Genesis 22:17.

name increases in the earth through the increase in a godly family. Generation after generation builds the name of God in the earth. Jesus was the firstborn of many sons.[94] We are true sons and joint heirs[95] in that lineage through faith.

CLEANING YOUR OWN WELLS

It appalls me when I see people who are supposed to be God's children, carrying His name, defaming Him and shaming His name by their actions. Do you realize that your rebellion embarrasses your heavenly Father as well as your natural and spiritual father?

Rebels against ***God, our Father***	*"They assemble together for grain and new wine, They rebel against Me; Though I disciplined and strengthened their arms, Yet they devise evil against Me; They return, but not to the Most High."* [96]

The name of the Most High will be great on the earth through His people, but the spread of His name is hindered when rebellious sons put their heavenly Father and their earthly fathers in a negative light. It grieves the Father when one of His choice sons or daughters is caught in some scandalous mess that is then publicized in the media.

Doesn't it bring shame to the name of God when you hear about a known Christian who robs a bank or shoots somebody? Inevitably, someone will say, "Oh, my! He was a Christian!" You are more appalled when you hear a negative news report about a Christian who has done something wrong because you know it brings reproach to your Father. Your Father's name is injured because someone didn't conduct himself in a godly manner.

---

[94] See Romans 8:29.
[95] See Romans 8:17.
[96] Hosea 7:14-16.

| David wept over the death of his rebellious son | *"Then the king was deeply moved, and went up to the chamber over the gate, and wept. And as he went, he said thus: 'O my son Absalom—my son, my son Absalom—if only I had died in your place! O Absalom my son, my son!' "* [97] |

David was tremendously grieved by the actions of his son Absalom, whom he loved so much. Absalom tried to take the kingdom away from his father David. He was a rebel. God has rebels in His family. Even though Absalom was a rebel, David loved him and grieved for him greatly.

Before David, Eli, the priest, had two sons. God killed both of those sons because they were an embarrassment to Him.

You and I can bring down the name of God, but we can also raise His name up. We like it when a celebrity or athlete stands up and says something about God. We didn't know they were a Christian, and they receive an award for something and give glory to Jesus. I'm not talking about the ones who just talk about giving Him thanks and do ungodly things in their songs and movies, but those who are living godly lives and then they are open about giving Him praise.

Your well can be free of dishonor toward your father. When you dishonor your father, making light of his words and work, you have become like the Philistines, kicking dirt into wells that were dug for your benefit. We live in a society that dishonors the Ten Commandments, but it is more important than ever to remember to "Honor your father and your mother, that your days may be long upon the land which the LORD your God is giving you." [98] *Spiritual leaders too.*

Your well can be free of the flesh life. Through carelessness, lack of self-discipline and neglect of prayer, you

---

[97] 2 Samuel 18:33.
[98] Exodus 20:12.

can allow carnality to pollute the waters in your belly that should be flowing with purity. Yet by the same token, when you are careful and self-disciplined, you can ensure that these waters stay fresh.

Your well can be free of quarreling and strife. When Isaac found the wells of his father, they had been rendered useless because the Philistines had filled them with dirt. Even when Isaac's herdsmen dug new wells, "The herdsmen of Gerar quarreled with Isaac's herdsmen, saying, 'The water is ours.' So he called the name of the well *Esek,* because they quarreled with him." [99] Today many homes are full of strife and bickering. I thank God for the past 33 years since my wife and I became Christians there has not been violence or strife in our home. I thank God that I don't have to live in that environment of always having to fight. That's hell on earth. Your well can be free of that deception and strife.

Your well can be free of deception. The word *Esek* means oppression, strife, violence; to oppress, to defraud, and to deceive. Many of us deceive one another. We deceive ourselves. You can be free of that in Christ.

Your well can be free of hostility. The Bible says that Isaac's workers dug another well, and they quarreled over that one, too. So he called its *Sitnah. Sitnah* means accusation, hatred, or contention. It means to lie in wait, an ambushment. It means to be an adversary. It means hostility. Your well can be free of that. [100]

Your well can be free of bitterness. The Bible says that when bitterness comes in, it rises up and defiles many. [101] Bitterness doesn't just affect you. It affects your children. It affects your house. It affects your neighbor. It affects everybody around you. Your husband or wife is suffering

---

[99] Genesis 26:20.
[100] Genesis 26:20-21.
[101] Hebrews 12:15.

because of your bitterness. You can be free of it.

Your well can be free of jealousy. Isaac was the son of promise. Ishmael was the son of Abraham's flesh, and his descendants have been jealous of his inheritance ever since. They are rebels who have chosen a different path. They don't bring honor to the name of their father. They don't honor their father's God. They didn't drink from their father's well. They don't drink from Jesus' wells of living water.

At the Temple Mount in Jerusalem the Muslims have inscribed the words that Allah has no son. They deny the deity of Jesus, the Son of God, because their god is not the real God. Allah is a demonic figure. Out of their rebellion and their wounding from being removed out of the lineage of God's plan, they are recipients of Ishmael's seed. You can trace that lineage all the way back to a tree with a little boy crying under it. The descendants of Ishmael have done evil because of that son's jealousy of the son called Isaac, the son of promise who went looking for his father's wells.

Your well can be free of hidden poison. One of the most dangerous things about poisoned wells is that the water can still look perfectly clean. A person can attend church, say all the right things, serve in all the right ways, but still poison those who drink from his life.

Your well can be free of hate. You can hate somebody and they can repent and go to heaven even if they've done something to you, but you will be the one who goes to hell, not them. The murderer on death row who repents and gets saved before God will go to heaven. You can have your bitterness and anger and hate. You can hate your mother or your father. You can hate your boss, your husband, or your wife. You can hate your dog. All that hatred will eat you up like cancer. You might say to me, "You don't know what they did to me." I know what my God did, and I know what Jesus did. He paid it all. He's the One who suffered. You have never suffered like that. You've never been on a cross. You've never had nails put through your hands. You've never had a crown of thorns on your head. Whatever they did, they didn't put you on a cross, but they put Him there and He already died for all that they did and all that you did.

WHAT CLEAN WELLS CAN DO

What happened at Calvary superseded all of my disappointments. Jesus cleansed my wells with His blood. He gave His blood and it washed me clean. I got saved. Born again. Washed in the blood. Cleansed by the living fountain.

Clean wells represent unending spiritual and natural wealth. Jesus said, "If anyone thirsts, let him come to Me and drink. He who believes in Me, as the Scripture has said, out of his heart will flow rivers of living water." [102] Wells of living water are wells that keep flowing and producing from generation to generation.

Clean wells represent something lasting. When Isaac went looking for his father's wells, he knew that he would find them because wells represent something lasting that we inherit from our spiritual fathers and pass on to our sons after us. They represent those inner reserves of refreshing from the Lord from which generations of spiritual flocks can drink.

How do we seek the wells of our fathers? We search out their teachings and the legacy of their character with diligence and zeal.

Isaac didn't find the wells by taking a casual glance around. He had to search them out. We find the wells of our fathers by paying attention to their words and preserving their work and honoring the significance of their lives and ministry. You see, God will bless you for your father's sake. That's why

---

[102] John 7:37-39.

you'd better not despise your father.

Clean wells provide a place of rest. When you seek out the well of your father, the God of that well will show up and bless you and your descendents. When Isaac finally found a well that he didn't have to fight over, he pitched a tent and set up camp there. Then the Lord told him that He would bless him and multiply his seed for his father Abraham's sake.

Clean wells can be enlarged. When you have a Rehoboth well, it means you've got room, and you find room for more. As Jabez said, "Lord, enlarge my territory. God, make me bigger." [103]

Clean wells have enough water for everyone. The bigger God makes your well, the more water comes in. It starts to spill over and you have room for blacks and room for whites. You have room for those of every color. Rehoboth was a wide place with room for all.

Clean wells replace problems with blessings. The greater God becomes in your life, the smaller your problems and the greater your blessings become. You can reach out and forgive. You can show mercy. You can say, "You know what? It doesn't matter anymore. I need to get past this problem in my life." You have room for that grandmother, sister, brother, doctor, or somebody else you don't like. There's room in the kingdom of God when you have a clean well.

Clean wells give you joy. God wants to make you bigger than the mess that you were holding onto that brought dirt into your wells. He wants to make you bigger than that little foolish grudge. Pity parties and pouting don't appeal to you any more because your well has given you joy. "Therefore, with joy you will draw water from the wells of

---

[103] See 1 Chronicles 4:10.

salvation." [104] When you're saved, water comes out of the wells of your salvation. Joy is inside of you, bubbling up and overflowing because the debris is gone.

Clean wells are reservoirs for you to share with others. I haven't met a flock yet that knew how to draw water from a well on its own. The job of a herdsman, like Isaac, was to draw water for the flock. Remember, the well is a reservoir. The entire point of a well is that when there hasn't been rain in 100 days, the flock can still come to you to find water because you have access to a well. Drawing water is most often expressed through serving, tirelessly, day in and day out, yet it doesn't have to be a chore. When you keep that well open and stay clean, you'll find that something phenomenal begins to happen. You'll find that the life, the blessing, the anointing, indeed, everything you need, is readily available.

Clean wells provide water in times of war. When you are supplying the next generation with life, all of a sudden the waters of heaven begin to flood your well. You don't know what tomorrow will bring, because life has a way of throwing unexpected curveballs. You have to be able to draw water when you need it.

I have been in so many situations where I thanked God that I didn't have to clean my well, on the spot, to get the resource for that moment. It's hard to clean the house and serve company at the same time. It's hard to clean wells and fight a war at the same time. The Lord gave us a secret weapon for the spiritual wars to come. If we find the wells, clean them, and preserve them, when war comes, we can draw from them all that we need.

PRESERVING THE WELLS

We can preserve the wells of our fathers even as we

---

[104] Isaiah 12:3.

keep digging new wells ourselves. When we preserve what was completed before our time, we demonstrate that we understand the true value of the water that lies underneath. Those who understand the value of their fathers' wells can preserve those rich sources of water for generations.

Preserve your wells through diligence. Wells are dug through dirt, and dirt often finds its way back in. In your inner wells, the dirt of the flesh-life can creep into our reserves of holiness. Stay diligent about the condition of your well.

Continually dig your wells deeper through prayer. I have friends with deep wells who don't sleep in the night. They sleep in the day because they pray all night. The more you pray, the deeper you get.

People who don't pray have shallow wells. Shallow Christians are people who don't pray. They have no well in them. There's no reservoir left where they can pull out something of the wealth that they used to walk in. The living water isn't there any more. They're empty. They have about a cup of water instead of a full well. After they drink the cup, they've got nothing left because they have no prayer life.

You dig your well and keep your well clean through prayer. The deeper you dig your well in prayer, the longer you will be able to survive a drought and still have plenty. If your well has been vandalized, as Isaac's wells were, you may have to dig again by allowing God to do deeper works inside of you, pushing deeper in prayer and yielding yourself more to the Holy Spirit.

Stay in the place where you find a good well. Notice what Isaac did. When he found the well he needed, he pitched his tent. He said, "This is the spot where there's a free flowing well. I'm going to plant myself here, because everything around me can benefit from this well." He had been a nomad herdsman, but he knew that when he found water he should stop moving and settle down. I was saved 33 years ago and stayed in that one church. I've been to only two churches in my life. The church I got saved in and this church where I am now. I pitched my tent and got planted. Is this a good church? Yes. Has it got problems? Of course. They're called people. You're a problem. I'm a problem. But Jesus is a Solver of problems. I planted my tent because there is water in this well. People get saved and delivered, and meet God. There's a free-flowing well in this house and God's anointing flows.

Reactivate your well continually with your words. One day God commanded Moses to do something unusual. He said, "Moses, when it's been a tough day, go over to the well and sing to it. Sing to the well, 'Spring up, O well!' " [105] Sometimes you've got to look at your well and say, "Hey! Well! Listen to me! I will serve the Lord. I will rejoice in my God." You start to sing and all of a sudden the well opens up. Joy comes out. Bubbling flows out. Healing flows out.

| **Speak to the well in song— Spring up!** | *"From there they went to Beer, which is the well where the Lord said to Moses, 'Gather the people together, and I will give them water.' Then Israel sang this song:* " 'Spring up, O well! " 'All of you sing to it.' " [106] |

You've got to admit that probably looked pretty strange, yet it tells us something important. Even an inner well in good repair will be activated by your mouth. The anointing of God is in you, but it's not *of you*; it's *of God*. That word "spring" means to stir up.

You have to stir up the dirt in the well and keep removing the dirt until the water bubbles over and flows out of your well and there's purity again, and righteousness again, and you don't miss what God is doing.

[105] See Numbers 21:17.
[106] Numbers 21:16-17.

Clean wells heal everything they touch. When you rejoice and sing into your well, it bubbles up and overflows. The pure water begins to heal everything it touches. There's joy in your well, but you've got to sing to the well.

POWER OF ONE PERSON WITH A WELL

Every Christian has the potential of being that one person who changes the course of society from destruction and the devil to a journey to God and eternal life. You can't put your head in the sand and say, 'It doesn't matter," because it does matter. Going to church does matter. Serving God does matter. It does matter to stand up and make a difference.

By one man, Adam, sin entered into the world,[107] and, by one man, Jesus, righteousness overcame that sin.[108] One man can make a difference. You can become that one who makes a difference. Abraham was one man, and God called him His friend.[109] His life made a difference. His son's life made a difference. His spiritual and natural prosperity were passed on.

Inherited prosperity of Isaac, son of Abraham, a friend of God	*"Then Isaac sowed in that land, and reaped in the same year a hundredfold; and the Lord blessed him. The man began to prosper, and continued prospering until he became very prosperous."* [110]

Notice that when you have access to your father's wealth, God doesn't just make you prosperous. He makes you continue to prosper, and then He makes you *very* prosperous. You even become the envy of unbelievers.

---

[107] See Romans 5:12.
[108] See Romans 5:16.
[109] See James 2:23.
[110] Genesis 26:12-13.

Envied by enemies because of possessions	*". . . for he had possessions of flocks and possessions of herds and a great number of servants. So the Philistines envied him."* [111]

The Philistines envied the wealth of Isaac because of his great possessions. It will be a great day when the world starts to envy the Church instead of the Church envying the world. When Christians are that rich, they will no longer be saying, "Boy, I wish we were like them. I wish we had the money they have. I wish we could do what they do." God is going to turn that around. Can He do it through you?

SONS JUST LIKE GOD, OUR FATHER

When we realize that greater is He that is in us than he that is in the world,[112] we will begin to use the Father's resources to do greater works in every generation.

I have two sons. When they were growing up they wanted to do everything I did. If I got a hammer, the next thing you knew, they would get a hammer, especially my younger son. I had to monitor him because he had an affection for tools. Mine. When he was just four or five years old he would open my tool box and help himself to my tools. When I went looking for them, they were missing. Maybe he needed to readjust a plastic model so he grabbed a 22-ounce hammer. With one blow he customized the entire model.

I would find screwdrivers lying outside in the yard where he had attempted to unscrew something that was mounted to the side of the house—like the gutter. I would find my tools in strange places and I would know that my little guy had been there.

When he was still small I could say to him, "Go get me a Phillips head screwdriver." He would walk right over and

---

[111] Genesis 26:14.
[112] See 1 John 4:4.

pick it out. There might be ten screwdrivers in the bag, but he would pull out the one with a Phillips head. I would tell him to get me a pair of needle nose pliers. He'd get me the pliers with the skinny little nose. He knew those tools, just like his father.

> *When a father does something, a son wants to*
> *emulate him. He wants to please him. Even*
> *when there is no real father-son relationship,*
> *sons still try to please their fathers.*

Before the beginning of time, God desired a family. His heart's desire is to have mature sons and daughters who willingly choose to love Him and put Him first in every area of their lives. God's Son came as the firstborn Son among many sons. We are sons. When we become like Him, the name of God is increased.

You may have dishonored your father or rebelled against him. Maybe your wells were stopped up with fear, or doubt, or unbelief. You had debris inside of you that hindered you from flowing in Christ-likeness. It might have been religious debris or the debris of false teaching. Maybe it was bitterness or jealousy. Say, *"God, release me from that dirt inside of me. Release your power. I want to be just like You."*

Called the Sons of God

"Behold, what manner of love the Father hath bestowed upon us, that we should be called the sons of God: therefore the world knoweth us not, because it knew him not. Beloved, now are we the sons of God, and it doth not yet appear what we shall be: but we know that, when he shall appear, we shall be like him; for we shall see him as he is." [113]

Dig deeper by prayer and dig your well clean. Pray until you pray through and your well is clean, then keep your

---

[113] 1 John 3:1-2 KJV.

65

well clean.

> *God's name will be made great through sons*
> *and daughters who want to please Him. The*
> *greatness of His name will be increased*
> *numerically as born-again believers multiply*
> *and give honor to His name.*

Wells tap into unseen rivers underground. When the water flows, you can have so much water that it's like a river. With that living water released and flowing through you, everywhere you go, you carry healing. You carry a river, and everything you touch will be affected by that river. You get in and it's up to your ankles, then your knees, then your thighs. Then you're swimming in the river of God.[114]

There's a river flowing. Get in it. Don't let your flesh keep you away from it. Get in the river. Don't let your mind keep you from God. Don't let your attitude separate you from Him. If your faith has fallen down, let faith arise in you. Believe God and get in the river. Don't be self-conscious. Be God-conscious. If you need to deal with any of these areas, you can do it now. Be conscious of God alone.

---

[114] See Ezekiel 47.

66

CHAPTER 6

GETTING IN THE FLOW OF THE ANOINTING

"It is like the precious ointment upon the head,
that ran down upon the beard, even Aaron's beard:
that went down to the skirts of his garments." [115]

One day, two sons stepped in front of their father as he was preparing to go into the presence of God. The two boys said, "Dad's busy. We'll help him." They got some strange coals and put them in the fire on the altar. The minute they did that, God killed them on the spot. The two boys fell over dead, and the Bible says that God did not allow Aaron to grieve or to go to the funeral of his sons. [116]

What happened? The boys got in front of their father, the one whom God had called to be the head over them. They did not follow God's protocol. They thought that the anointing could flow up from them to their father, instead of flowing down from the father to his sons. They tried to place themselves outside of the structure established by God. They got out of the flow of the anointing.

---

[115] Psalm 133:2 NKJV.
[116] See Leviticus 10.

Psalm 133 speaks of the flow of the anointing oil from Aaron's head, to his beard, to the hem of his garment. Whenever the sequence of head to hem is out of order, the body is out of alignment, and it's crippled. Crippled people[117] were not allowed into the presence of God in the Old Testament. God would not receive them.

> *In order to receive the power of God,*
> *you have to follow the order of God.*
> *That requires humility.*

Before God will lift you up, you have to go down and humble yourself in the sight of the Lord.

God resists the proud, but gives grace to the humble	*"Yes, all of you be submissive to one another, and be clothed with humility, for* *"'God resists the proud,* *"'But gives grace to the humble.'* *"Therefore humble yourselves under the mighty hand of God, that He may exalt you in due time."* [118]

In Moses' day, when Korah and his friends rebelled against him as their leader, the earth swallowed them. What had they done? They had said, "Look, Moses, we can hear from God just as well as you can." [119] They got out of line with their pride, and God Himself judged them.

THE FLOW OF GOD'S ANOINTING IS DOWNWARD

If you force your way up when God is telling you to go down, you're going against the current of God's flow. You'll encounter resistance, because God's flow is downward. You

---

[117] See Leviticus 21:21 and other references.
[118] 1 Peter 5:5-6 NKJV.
[119] See Numbers 16.

have to learn how to get in that flow to receive His power.

Let's go back to Psalm 133. It's very important to our understanding of the flow of God's anointing.

Oil of anointing runs down from the head to the hem

"Behold, how good and how pleasant it is
For brethren to dwell together in unity!
It is like the precious oil upon the head,
Running down on the beard,
The beard of Aaron,
Running down on the edge of his garments.

"It is like the dew of Hermon,
Descending upon the mountains of Zion;
For there the Lord commanded the blessing—
Life forevermore." [120]

The dew of Mount Hermon is more than 9,000 feet in the air. Mount Hermon is the highest mountain around. When I was in Israel, I could see it from the Dead Sea, even though it was miles away. The dew from melting snow at the top of Mount Hermon flows down into the Jordan River, continually building up volume. The Jordan River flows to the Sea of Galilee, where the water is 1,300 feet deep. Then the Jordan flows down into the Dead Sea. By this time, the rate of flow is 6 million tons of water every 24 hours. That's heavy dew!

The Bible says that the anointing is like the dew on the mountain that joins a river and becomes millions of tons of water at one of the places on earth, the Dead Sea. When you force your way to the top, all you get is dew. When you stay in a low place, you get 6 million tons of anointing.

The greatest anointing comes at the lowest level. The woman with the issue of blood who saw Jesus and reached out for Him in the crowd didn't try to touch His head. She touched the place of greatest anointing—the hem of His garment.

If you think the anointing is good on top of Mount

---

[120] Psalm 133:1-3 NKJV.

Hermon, think about what happened to that woman who touched His hem and got healed after all those years.

Healed by touching the hem of Jesus' garment	*"And suddenly, a woman who had a flow of blood for twelve years came from behind and touched the hem of His garment. For she said to herself, "If only I may touch His garment, I shall be made well." But Jesus turned around, and when He saw her He said, "Be of good cheer, daughter; your faith has made you well." And the woman was made well from that hour." [121]*

Jesus knew how the anointing would flow. He knew that if you get in alignment with the Father and the Son, you receive power. When you receive power through alignment, you can do greater works than the Head, because you are in the flow of His anointing. Here's another reminder.

Those who follow after Jesus will do greater works than He did	*Jesus said, "Most assuredly, I say to you, he who believes in Me, the works that I do he will do also; and greater works than these he will do, because I go to My Father." [122]*

The greatest flow is found at the lowest place. God has worked it out so that He puts the dew on the head, then it runs down over the beard and onto the coat, then down to the hem of the garment.

Many church leaders at the top don't want those under them to have greater power than they do, but I do. I understand that all I have is dew. Others under me will have a greater flow than I do because they are at the hem of the garment.

---

[121] Matthew 9:20-22 NKJV.
[122] John 14:12 NKJV.

70

If you don't want to remain in your assigned
place in the body of Christ and you try to reach
the head first, you're bypassing God's
protocol. You're trying to get the dew at the top
when you could have the deluge at the bottom.

Jesus said that if you want to be great in the kingdom, you become the least,[123] but leaders today don't want to go down to the hem to receive glory. They want to stay on top so they can keep the dew. They don't understand that the purpose of their ministry is to empower the people under them whom they father.

You cannot be a true father unless you
passionately desire to see those under you
flowing in a greater anointing than yours.

Are you in line for the power to fall on you, and then through you to others, or are you out of line?

POWER OF A SONSHIP RELATIONSHIP

Power comes through the garment of the father. The garment is sonship. When you have a sonship relationship with your father, you can flow in his anointing. When you don't wear a father's garment, you can't be a father's son. You can't get in the flow of his power, and you can't release power to others under you because you don't understand the flow.

Many people who attend church today don't want to be sons. They want to be gypsies, flitting from church to church.

Constantly changing churches is a dangerous lifestyle for you and everybody around you. As long as you're running back and forth, checking out preachers and visiting various meetings, you will never become anybody's son.

---

[123] See Luke 9:48.

71

When you find the house where God wants you,
He'll make you a son, and finally all of the
desires that you've had will come to pass in
sonship. God will start to use you
as the son of your father.

Come home to the Church

Everybody says they need fathers, but in the Church you hear,
"I don't want you to be my father. I want to find my own
father." Do you know what you need to do? Go to a church
and stay there. Submit yourself to a father who can make you
a great son through your obedience. You won't get the
garment of favor without a relationship with your father. The
garment doesn't come from being at the right meeting. It
comes from faithful sonship in the house of your father.

You say, "I'm going to do what I want to, when I want
to do it." Not if you want to grow up from a child state to a
mature Christian who can fulfill the will of God. You need a
father today so you can become a father.

Come to church. Have somebody lay hands on
you and set you in place and help you to relate
to the plan of God so that the anointing can
flow down to you and through you to become a
flood that washes the generation.

It's time to come home. Some of you need to come
home to the Father's house. You need to get back into a
father-son relationship.

My prayer for you

Father, I'm going to stop and pray for them right now. You
know who they are. You know what You're saying to them.
Break their hearts, O God. Break every stubborn spirit that's
in them, every stubborn mind that says, "I want to be my own
person." Show them the heart of a father so that they can go
to the hem of his garment and get in the flow of his anointing.
Then give them the heart of a father for others who need them.

In Jesus' name. Amen.

GOD DECIDES THE FLOW OF POWER

The power of God works in a flow that He has established. It's not a random bolt of lightning. We may not always understand why things happen as they do, but God does. God has spiritual and natural principles that He doesn't violate. He has established a flow, in earth as it is in heaven. He always knows what's going on. The flow has nothing to do with us; it has to do with God and His will. If you want to get the power, you have to get in the flow.

Whenever you see a preacher who falls, it isn't always the devil. He might have gotten out of the flow of God's power from becoming uncovered.

Sometimes in the Bible men got out of order and God killed them. He killed two sons of Aaron because they put the wrong coals on the fire, and He will also act now upon the principle that you're not going to step into the things of God when you're out of line with your head.

In the early Church, God established lines for the flow of power by setting up a governmental structure that flowed from Jesus to the apostles. Before He ascended, Jesus told them to wait for the promise and they would be endued with the power.

Jesus promised to empower us	*"Behold, I send the Promise of My Father upon you; but tarry in the city of Jerusalem until you are endued with power from on high."* [124]

Jesus is the head of the Church. He promised His disciples that they would be empowered by the Holy Spirit.

---

[124] Luke 24:49 NKJV.

When you're continually being battered around
and beaten up and destroyed and you never get
ahead, you've got to stop and say,
"How am I relating to the body of Christ?
Am I out of line?
Am I intolerant of God's timetable?"

Many of today's Christians would not have had the personal discipline to follow Jesus' instructions to tarry in the upper room. They would not have been willing to sit in submission to the leaders whom Jesus had left in place in headship over them long enough to wait for the power that came at Pentecost.

The Father's promise brought the release of power. If you don't have the release of God's power in your life, maybe you have not been patient regarding the conditions of the promise. Some of the blessings of the Father's promises have conditions.

If you were in ministry and now you're not, or you used to be on fire and now you're not on fire, or whatever your situation is, stop and say, "Wait a minute. Am I out of line?"

God's anointing on people follows a flow that's as fixed as the law of gravity. Have you ever heard of pouring oil on someone's knees and it flows upward to the head? It never happens. If you want to get in the flow, do you go over the head? Of course not! If you want to get in the flow, do you sever yourself from the body? Of course you don't.

Can you imagine seeing anointing oil poured on someone's head, and then a severed hand crawls over to try to get in on the action? It would freak you out. Any body parts not lined up with the head won't last long. The body can survive without the arm, but the arm can't survive without the body.

You need to be in order more than
the order needs you.

Getting in line with the principle of fathering is key to being part of this outpouring of the power of God. This business of spiritual fatherhood is not a minor thing in the Kingdom of God. It is absolutely key to seeing the power of God poured out in our generation as never before.

GOING AFTER MORE GREATNESS

Most Christians know that we could use more of God in our society. We are getting signals that an outpouring greater than we've ever seen is coming, but it is absolutely essential that you embrace this principle of fathering if you are going to be a part of it, and if you want the fruit of that outpouring to remain after you're gone.

Unfortunately, I still see around me almost entirely the opposite. I see a Church that is full of immature, selfish people, and a society that is following in its footsteps. I didn't think I'd ever live in a world where we would sue a restaurant for serving us junk food, when we knew good and well what it was when we bought it. We've got immature old people and immature young people—the blind leading the blind.

When I got saved, I came out of a life of gang-fights and crime. I understood the power of Satan, and I understood the incredible need for the power of God in my life. I knew how powerless I was on my own, because I had had a taste of what Satan could do to me.

> *When I found a spiritual father, I ran to him and I stayed under his covering to become a man of God who received his power the right way, under divine order. Then I could become a faithful father to others.*

When you desire the power of God because you truly understand how much you need it for yourself and society and those you will father, you're on the right track to receive it. That's why I could stay up night after night, praying and

75

seeking God for His power, and He honored that.

Enlightened understanding

If you are simply hungry for power, and think because you call yourself a Christian that God's power is at your disposal, you are in grave danger. Lots of Christians want power for its own sake; they are being set up to accept Satan's power in disguise. They need God's wisdom and revelation. They need their understanding to be enlightened.

Look at what Paul says about our great inheritance of wisdom and revelation from the Father:

Exceeding greatness of God—His inheritance given to the saints and His power that is not yet fully released

". . . that the God of our Lord Jesus Christ, the Father of glory, may give to you the spirit of wisdom and revelation in the knowledge of Him, the eyes of your understanding being enlightened; that you may know what is the hope of His calling, what are the riches of the glory of His inheritance in the saints, and what is the exceeding greatness of His power toward us who believe, according to the working of His mighty power which He worked in Christ when He raised Him from the dead and seated Him at His right hand in the heavenly places, far above all principality and power and might and dominion, and every name that is named, not only in this age but also in that which is to come. And He put all things under His feet, and gave Him to be head over all things to the church, which is His body, the fullness of Him who fills all in all." [125]

Paul, one of the greatest men of God to walk the earth, is looking forward to greater power being released. He is not

---

[125] Ephesians 1:17-23 NKJV.

talking about something that is just impressive. He is talking about *exceeding greatness*, because that is how great God is.

Desire for greatness

Mankind has a deep-seated desire to achieve greatness. Every time an Olympic or other world record is set, we know that someone else will eventually come along and break it. That is our nature. We try to top what was done before.

Now how could the true Great One, God Himself, be any different? In fact, He is the One Who defines greatness, and He has chosen to do it through the Church.

God is waiting to break His own records through you. Your future is not ahead of you, it's in you because God is in you.

ANOINTING FOLLOWS CONSISTENCY

I want to show you how to get in on the greatness of God for yourself and others by going to Joel chapter 2.

Sons and daughters shall prophesy

"And it shall come to pass afterward That I will pour out My Spirit on all flesh; Your sons and your daughters shall prophesy, Your old men shall dream dreams, Your young men shall see visions. And also on My menservants and on My maidservants I will pour out My Spirit in those days." [126]

Look at the use of the term sons and daughters. It does not say, "Your church members shall prophesy." It certainly doesn't say, "Your wandering nomads who have visited seven churches in the last year will prophesy." It says your sons and

---

[126] Joel 2:28-29 NKJV.

77

daughters will prophesy.

You will remember we discussed the anointed garments of favor, passed from father to son. For priests, the anointing was poured on these garments, not on the man himself. This helped the people to understand that there was nothing particularly special about this individual person. It was the garment he was wearing. It was that garment that was transferred, and the anointing with it.

You might think that catching the anointing has to do with being in the right meeting, so you travel around to hear different speakers—even on Sunday mornings—who are supposed to be good. Actually, the Bible says that getting the anointing has to do with our position as a son or a daughter. That speaks of consistency and placement in the house of a father.

Why are so many Christians living powerless lives of malnutrition, starvation and debt? It's not because there aren't enough good meetings. They've been to all the meetings, yet they're barely getting by. They barely have a prayer life, barely read the Scriptures, barely have faith. Every day is a struggle. Every day they're beat up by the devil, yet they supposedly serve this powerful God.

If you won't line up in your position as a son or a daughter, you will miss the power of God in your life the way He wants you to have it.

I've prayed for people who were born with legs going the wrong way, or they had a broken back, and I have seen God heal them. I prayed for a girl who had no irises in her eyes, and they grew back in front of me. I would have no business trying to teach you anything about the power of God if it were not operating in my own life. I didn't receive the power of God in my life by wandering around like a spiritual gypsy, looking for the next great meeting. I grew by being planted. I'm still planted, and my roots go down deep.

Harlotry in the Church

I believe one of the reasons that pornography has become such a plague in our generation is that the church herself is a harlot. She has discarded the covering of authority and is selling herself to appease men's flesh. We've got to restore power to the Church by restoring purity to the Church. We need the anointing of our fathers who were righteous men of God.

A businessman who didn't know God told me he saw that those women are desperate to find a right relationship with a man, a real father, and that's why they do that. Can they find real fathers in the church today?

The pimps and pornographers in the inner cities would have no power if the Church were in its proper place. They deal in uncovered women, but they are actually showing up an uncovered Church. The Church is a woman and she's uncovered. She's selling services that appease men but don't call them to account.

FEELING THE WEIGHT OF POWER

Saints, we don't have to be rocket scientists to figure this out. You get the coat on. Six million tons of anointing from the dew. The power of God hasn't ceased. God's power is available to everybody.

If the power is there, and you don't have it, you need to find out why.

If you're no longer satisfied with little meals of scraps and struggling along with no energy, you can release the power to raise the dead, live a victorious life, and get rid of the spiritual numbness in your brain that makes you walk around in a daze. Our God is a God of exceeding greatness, and He wants to show His greatness through you.

Prayer of humility

"Father, forgive me for being out of line. Forgive me for getting out of alignment and trying to bypass Your order and not wear the coat of my father. Forgive me. Put me in a place

*where I can relate to a father. Give me a father's heart. Give
me a heart to return to my father. May Your Church today
represent Your heart. In Jesus' name. Amen."*

We have many obstacles ahead in the journey to
restore fatherhood and sonship to the Church, but we can win.
I will show you some of the obstacles that I see, and present a
plan for getting past them to a place of greatness for this hour.

SECTION III.

ENTERING THE
WORLD OF FATHERING

CHAPTER 7

FINAL OBSTACLES TO SONSHIP

*"For the earnest expectation of the creation
eagerly waits for the revealing of the sons of God."* [127]

D id you ever notice what happens when two people get married after they already have some age on them? They are set in their ways. They know where they want to keep the toothpaste. They even know the right way to squeeze it. The toilet paper must be rolled out this way and not that way.

Some ladies marry a knucklehead whose socks can stand up by themselves. He could just jump his feet in there and run. If she says something about it, he says, "Hey, what do you mean? Don't touch them. That's my favorite pair of socks."

Then he always wears his favorite T-shirt. It's so favorite that it's carrying the stains from pizza he ate about three weeks ago. It isn't a favorite to anybody else, but it is to him. He didn't marry her so that she could interfere with his habits.

The same thing happens when a man marries a lady

---

[127] Romans 8:19.

who has collected 10,000 pieces of make-up. She is trying to fix what, at this point, may not be able to be fixed, but because it was on sale and it was something new that was guaranteed to take away wrinkles, she bought some of it. When he goes to find room to brush his teeth, he can't even find the sink. It's somewhere under the hair dryers—plural. He puts his hand down on something and he gets burned. He used to keep his shaver on the sink, and that was it. Hopefully he had some deodorant, but nothing else.

My point is that when two independent people get married they stumble over obstacles that get in the way of blending their two lives into one another and building a godly family that lasts. If they are mature Christians, they get past those things and grow together gracefully by giving up pride and their little habits that have nothing to do with what is really important in life. They see the big picture—that God has called them to be together for His destiny and purpose. In coming together, they are changed. By giving up something, they are gaining so much more from their unity and commitment to seeing one another increase in God.

INDEPENDENT MEMBER MEETS SPIRITUAL FATHER

When independent people come into a church relationship, they face some of the same obstacles to their own growth. All of their lives, even in church, they have protected themselves, promoted themselves, and done everything that was focused on self, self, self. They have learned that they can join a church and choose a favorite place to sit—then attend on Sunday just long enough to say they have been to church. They may participate in some social activities or even help out, but you never get to know them. The concept of yielding to someone in leadership has never entered their minds. What? Somebody I hardly know, and who doesn't know me?

When you have an independent spirit, it's hard for you to come into a church family that has a structure and a father figure who is saying this is what we do here and this is what we don't do here. It means you might have to give up your independent spirit. You might have to become vulnerable.

When people don't understand that God has established sonship and fatherhood in the Church as a means for helping people to come of age, they stumble over the obstacles without seeing the benefits. They have just found a spiritual family that can make a difference in their lives, but they still want to squeeze the toothpaste the same way. They don't want to hear about their dirty T-shirt.

Growing up as a faithful son under his father

Maturity in Christ comes as a result of unity and sonship under a faithful father. The Apostle Paul wrote about the character qualities that his spiritual son Timothy developed under his training:

Timothy's proven character as a son with his father, Paul

> *"But I trust in the Lord Jesus to send Timothy to you shortly, that I also may be encouraged when I know your state. For I have no one like-minded, who will sincerely care for your state. For all seek their own, not the things which are of Christ Jesus. But you know his proven character, that as a son with his father he served with me in the gospel."* [128]

Timothy is a role model for sons and daughters growing up in the church, including those like Timothy who had no natural father imparting the Gospel to them. Paul speaks of the godliness of Timothy's mother and grandmother, but Timothy's father isn't mentioned. Timothy broke the fatherless curse and found a father in Paul.

Here are some of the character qualities that Paul mentioned that developed in his son Timothy:

---

[128] Philippians 2:19-23.

85

- Like-minded with his spiritual father, Paul
- Sincerely caring for the people in the local church
- Focused on Jesus Christ instead of himself
- Possessing proven character
- Behaving like a son toward his father
- Serving in the Gospel alongside his father

Stumbling blocks from being offended
People who lack a good relationship with their fathers can grow, as Timothy did, but they have to work at overcoming their past experiences. They may have trouble trying to fit in to a church where there is a spiritual father and sonship is practiced. They just don't seem to get it, so they get offended. That's their exit strategy. If I get offended, I can leave. That's how they miss the blessings of sonship.

Relationships are difficult things to develop. They often produce offense. It seems as if all some people know is how to get offended. They wake up in the morning feeling offended. They're looking at everything that happens that day as a reason to get offended. It's a means of self protection.

In a real family, you get offended about every 16 minutes, give or take a few. You have no option but to get over it, suck it up, cook dinner when you should be throwing dinner on his head, crawl into bed with your enemy, and go and kiss those little sweet angels when you would like to hang them by their toes in the closet for at least an hour. But it's called family. In family, you just say, "All right. Round 2. Let's get ready to rumble." Right? The bell rings at 7 A.M. You jump out of bed ready to fight.

But somewhere along the way a miraculous thing happens. You—not they—get changed. To put it simply, you grow up.

Creation yearns for God's people to grow up
The Bible says that the whole earth yearns for mature sons of God to be revealed: "For the earnest expectation of the creation eagerly waits for the revealing of the sons of

86

God." [129] Sonship is a process of maturing into someone who can fulfill the expectations of all creation. Sons of God mature with a spiritual father to lead them. That's why God gave us the fivefold ministry—apostle, prophet, evangelist, pastor, teacher—for the perfecting of the saints for the work of the ministry—that we all might come to the full stature of maturity as sons of God.

Fivefold ministry helps bring saints to maturity	*"And he gave some, apostles; and some, prophets; and some, evangelists; and some, pastors and teachers; For the perfecting of the saints, for the work of the ministry, for the edifying of the body of Christ: Till we all come in the unity of the faith, and of the knowledge of the Son of God, unto a perfect man, unto the measure of the stature of the fulness of Christ." [130]*

God's ultimate purpose is to make us mature sons who represent Him in every way, just as Jesus did. Jesus said that "he that hath seen me hath seen the Father." [131]

HOW GOD'S NAME IS MADE GREAT

God's name shall be great among the nations	*" 'For from the rising of the sun, even to its going down, My name shall be great among the Gentiles;* *In every place incense shall be offered to My name, And a pure offering;* *For My name shall be great among the nations,' Says the Lord of hosts." [132]*

When Jesus did great things, He made His Father's

---

[129] Romans 8:19.
[130] Ephesians 4:11-13 KJV.
[131] John 14:9 KJV.
[132] Malachi 1:11.

name great in the earth. God's name shall be great among the nations. We love to declare that phrase as Christians, but what does it really mean? Does it mean that all of a sudden everyone will walk around saying "God! God!" all the time? Does it mean revival is going to break out? I don't think so. I don't think that it means either of those things.

As I mentioned earlier, the word "great" in this context means great in number, not just "mighty" or "impressive." The verses mean that God's name will be numerous in the earth.

One of many offspring. A man's name is made numerous by having many offspring. If you have a church where there is a family named Wesley with ten children and all of them have ten children, you can see how many Wesleys would be in your church. The name Wesley would be numerous and great in your church.

Builder of the family name. Recall that in the Bible the word "son" means "builder of the family name," or "builder of the nation."

> *God's name is made great on the earth through the multiplication of sons and daughters whose lives bring honor to His name. His name increases every day that born-again believers are added into the kingdom and become sons and daughters who rightly represent their Heavenly Father.*

Every day more Christians bearing the name of the Father expose the world to His greatness through their words and deeds.

Copying the Father. Jesus said that a characteristic of a son is to copy what he sees his father doing, and a characteristic of a father who loves his son is to show the son what he is doing so the son can copy him. Jesus used Himself as an example of how a son makes his father's name great.

88

| Jesus copying His Father | *"Most assuredly, I say to you, the Son can do nothing of Himself, but what He sees the Father do; for whatever He does, the Son also does in like manner. For the Father loves the Son, and shows Him all things that He Himself does."* [133] |

Jesus did whatever He saw the Father do, and Jesus was the firstborn among many sons.[134] We are the sons who followed Jesus, and we should be copying the Father just as Jesus did. God wants us to copy Him. He shows us His nature through His Word, through His fivefold ministry, and through our prayers and experiences with Him. Then He says, "Now act the way I do."

Honoring the father. A godly son brings honor to his earthly father and to God. When a known Christian falls into sin, or does something stupid or irresponsible, he profanes the name of the Lord[135] instead of making His name great. When David committed adultery with Bathsheba and then killed her husband, God sent the prophet Nathan to tell him that his actions had brought down the name of the Lord. The Lord exacted a penalty for this sin.

| David's actions brought shame to God's name | *"And Nathan said to David, 'The Lord also has put away your sin; you shall not die. However, because by this deed you have given great occasion to the enemies of the Lord to blaspheme, the child also who is born to you shall surely die.' Then Nathan departed to his house."* [136] |

---

[133] John 5:19-20.
[134] See Romans 8:29.
[135] See Malachi 1:12.
[136] 2 Samuel 12:13-15.

FOLLOWING YOUR SPIRITUAL FATHER

ɪɴ a spiritual family with a father like Elijah, a son recognizes and accepts his spiritual father into his life and grows up to be just like him. This takes time and considerable persistence. It's hard to do, because the son has to give up something to become like his father.

Following your father's agenda. A son has to change his agenda to fit his father's agenda. That's how he grows.

Elijah said to Elisha, "Do you want to be my son? You have asked a hard thing." Elijah called Elisha to be his spiritual son on the instruction of the Lord, but Elisha had to be persistent and pursue his father to stay in that position of sonship and learn everything that Elijah had to teach him. That was hard, because Elijah was testing him.

Running after your father. Elijah tried to leave him behind, but Elisha declared, "For as the LORD lives and as your soul lives, I will not leave you." [137]

> *When you are a son, you don't wait for your father to come running after you. You go running after him. That shows that you know you belong to him. It demonstrates your commitment to that relationship.*

Belonging to your father. Elisha made plain his commitment to his father when he said, "I'm not going to leave you. I want something from you. I want to be your son. I can't have a proper relationship of true sonship unless I stay connected to you. I need to belong to something." Elisha had parents. He wasn't looking for natural sonship. He was looking for spiritual sonship. That's where we need to keep our focus.

---

[137] 2 Kings 2:2.

90

Inheritance of a firstborn son. Remember that Elisha asked his father for a double portion. He was referring to the generational inheritance that belongs to a firstborn son. He was looking for approval. He was looking for someone to recognize him and stamp him with credibility so he could move forward in the spirit of Elijah. It's so easy for me to see this. Elisha was asking Elijah if he would become his spiritual father.

On your father's terms, not yours. Today many would-be Elishas have identified the need for an Elijah in their lives, but they have asked for this relationship on their own terms without accepting the process that qualifies them for the inheritance and the right to be called sons or daughters of this man.

One day I was at a political rally and I saw some young men who had passed through my church. I knew they wanted me to see them that day. They wanted me to approve them. For most of their lives there had been calamity after calamity, failure after failure. They were angry. They were out of order. They would abandon this, then run from that. They were looking for my approval, but they were not willing to submit to a father, so they developed an independent spirit. They wanted me to see them without being willing to follow me as a father.

The independent spirited person always wants
the father to see things the son's way.
That is an immature approach.
Mature sons don't do that.

If Elisha had an independent spirit, he would have expected Elijah to see things his way, but Elijah set the requirements. His son didn't set the requirements.

From Elijah's position as a father he said, "Do you want my double portion? All right. This is the requirement. If you see me when I'm going up, you shall receive it. If you don't see me, you won't get it."

Elijah set the conditions for his son Elisha to follow

"And so it was, when they had crossed over, that Elijah said to Elisha, 'Ask! What may I do for you, before I am taken away from you?'

"Elisha said, 'Please let a double portion of your spirit be upon me.'

"So he said, 'You have asked a hard thing. Nevertheless, if you see me when I am taken from you, it shall be so for you; but if not, it shall not be so.' " [138]

Elijah was saying, "Son, if you'll submit, if you'll see me as your father in the spirit, then I can transfer to you in the next realm what you need to be a son who can do what I do." The original Hebrew says that Elijah was saying, "If you see eye to eye with me, then you will get my mantle. If you come in agreement with me, then you'll get my blessing."

RUNNING PAST OBSTACLES TO SONSHIP

The Bible sometimes talks about the Christian life as a race. In this chapter we are talking about the final obstacles in the race to mature sonship. We have to see it as a race we must run to win so that revival will come and it will have a lasting impact on our nation and the world.

There is a finish line. The joy of the Lord is set before us. However, we must first run a race of endurance through obstacles.

We can prepare for the race that is set before us by understanding the obstacles we will face and the weights that could slow us down.

---

[138] 2 Kings 2:9-11.

Running the race with endurance, looking to Jesus

"Therefore we also, since we are surrounded by so great a cloud of witnesses, let us lay aside every weight, and the sin which so easily ensnares us, and let us run with endurance the race that is set before us, looking unto Jesus, the author and finisher of our faith, who for the joy that was set before Him endured the cross, despising the shame, and has sat down at the right hand of the throne of God. For consider Him who endured such hostility from sinners against Himself, lest you become weary and discouraged in your souls." [139]

Here are some forces in the Church and society today that sons will have to overcome in order to run well.

- Devaluation of manhood
- Half-hearted sacrifice by men
- Dealing treacherously in family and church
- Expecting benefits without accepting responsibility
- Information without accountability
- Distractions
- Hesitation
- Despising chastening and becoming illegitimate
- Building homes without fathers
- Rejecting family life
- Running away from spiritual churches
- Disrespect for God
- Disrespect for pastors
- Disrespect for fathers
- Telling your father what to say
- Telling your father what to do
- Youth ministries that produce rebels
- Preference for brothers instead of fathers

---

[139] Hebrews 12:1-3.

- Feminizing the Gospel
- Carrying weights
- Covering up

Devaluation of manhood. On television, in movies, and unfortunately, in many homes, a mother teaches by her actions that it's OK for the children to disrespect their father. Sure, we have a few violent fathers. We have fathers who are knuckleheads and need to be in jail. But don't you dare think they all fit in that category. We also have a generation of rebellious women. That's how organizations like NOW came about. We have entire groups that put down men in the name of protecting women: "I'm woman. I don't need you. I'm better than you are."

Many fatherless women have been taught from a young age that husbands aren't necessary for families. In fact, they may have been taught that affirming their womanhood means denying the value of manhood. In many circles, men are now considered luxuries, not leaders. Many of these women are reacting to the failures of men in their own lives. However, the curse of fatherlessness will be perpetuated until men and women alike uphold the honor of fathers.

Half-hearted sacrifice by sons. Before I was a Christian, I would cut flowers from other people's yards to appease my stepmother when I got in trouble. How does a parent feel when they receive an offering that has been stolen or found in the trash can? Yet we offer God those kinds of offerings all the time, and God says He will not accept them.

An obstacle to true sonship that may loom even larger than overt rebellion is half-hearted sacrifice in the service of God. That is what Malachi means when he talks about those who offer sacrifices that are torn, lame and sick.

94

Unacceptable sacrifices are evil

> *"And when you offer the blind as a sacrifice,*
> *Is it not evil?*
> *And when you offer the lame and sick,*
> *Is it not evil?"* [140]

The Bible calls men deceivers when they behave as if they are giving their best, but they are giving leftovers. This can be more treacherous than outright rebellion, because it gives the appearance of sonship without the fruit.

Dealing treacherously in family and church. Another obstacle to true sonship is disunity. All Christians are family. They have one Father, who is God, but the prophet Malachi asks, "Why do we deal treacherously with one another?"

Treacherous dealings

> *"Have we not all one Father? Has not one God created us? Why do we deal treacherously with one another By profaning the covenant of the fathers?"* [141]

Most of us know that honesty is a good idea, but do we see that it is absolutely essential to unity? Disunity hurts everyone. It weakens the impact of the Church. God is telling us in this verse that good sons who understand covenant will deal honestly with their brothers and sisters. They will build unity that honors the Father and legitimizes us as sons of one God and one spiritual father. Only a dysfunctional father wants to see his children fighting. A true father wants his children to love and support one another loyally. It takes work to keep unity in a family, let alone an entire church. However, our willingness to keep that unity provides the blessings of sonship and makes the Church a stronger force for change.

---

[140] Malachi 1:8.
[141] Malachi 2:10.

Expecting benefits without accepting responsibility.
Lots of people want to get help from the church anytime they
need it, but they don't want to make a covenant commitment
to anyone inside the church. They don't stick by their brothers
and sisters when there is a misunderstanding. They want the
benefits of covenant without the responsibility.

Information without accountability. When multitudes
of Christians are fed mainly by television, radio, and the
Internet, you have people with plenty of information about the
Bible but no accountability. This can also happen in churches
that lack fathering relationships. People start to believe that
because they can repeat the words they heard some preacher
say that they know everything that preacher knows. They
become deeply opinionated on spiritual things with no direct
knowledge or experience with God or His Word. They lack
the relational skills that are the core of Jesus' commandment
to love others as you love yourself.

Distractions. If the enemy can't stop you from taking
ground for the kingdom of God, he will do his best to annoy
you to the point of making you ineffective. One day my wife
went into the basement for a gardening tool and ran into a big
stash of cobwebs. She looked like she was doing some sort of
wild dance, waving them away, trying to get them out of her
hair and eyes. That's fine if you just need to find a gardening
tool once in a while, but can you imagine running a race like
that? Yet that is how many of us are running, so annoyed with
the little distractions in our lives that we forget where we are
going.

Hesitation. The enemy wants to keep you guessing and
hesitating. In sports, if you hesitate, the other team might
score. They call it choking. In baseball, when the batter
chokes, he waits too long to swing at the ball. In basketball, a
player goes in for a lay-up, but instead of making a shot, he
hesitates, and the other players block him before he can score.
You can have all the talent and ability in the world, but if you

haven't practiced keeping your focus, you will choke. A paralysis comes with every analysis. Before a basketball game, you have to prepare both physically and mentally. Why do we think the game of life in God is any different? We have to train our minds in advance to be ready to focus on God during times of challenge without hesitation.

Despising chastening and becoming illegitimate. The Bible warns that we must not despise correction, because only illegitimate sons are never corrected. Correction helps us to grow. We don't even have to agree that we need it. We honor the father who gives it by accepting the principle of correction first, then looking more closely at what he is saying. Chastening is something good. It is a demonstration of God's love and a father's love.

Don't be discouraged by rebukes	*"My son, do not despise the chastening of the Lord,* *Nor be discouraged when you are rebuked by Him;* *For whom the Lord loves He chastens,* *And scourges every son whom He receives."* [142]

You prove your sonship when you take chastening and love correction. You maintain a right attitude. A real father will not always be right, but your submission to him will be rewarded by God. He's the One you want to please, and He says you need to take what is being dished out by your father.

The Bible says that whom the Lord loves, He chastens. If you are without chastening in a church, then you are illegitimate and not a son.

The King James Version puts it in plain language. It says you're a bastard.

---

[142] Hebrews 12:5-6.

| *Those who can't be corrected are not sons* | *"But if ye be without chastisement, whereof all are partakers, then are ye bastards, and not sons."* [143] |

If nobody is disciplining you, you're not a son. You need to have somebody speaking into your life to be legitimate. And when he speaks, respect him.

| *Pay respect to those who correct you* | *"Furthermore, we have had human fathers who corrected us, and we paid them respect. Shall we not much more readily be in subjection to the Father of spirits and live?"* [144] |

Building homes without fathers. In the last 20 years in Baltimore and all over America I've seen the loss of fathers in a lot of homes. It's not just because there are more deadbeat dads. We have created a culture and developed a system that says that homes are better off without fathers. We will give you X amount of money if you don't have a man in the house. What is the girl going to do? She can make more money without a husband than she can with one.

In various ways, our society has perpetuated the curse of fatherlessness by allowing programs to take the place of fathers and providers for an entire generation. In an effort to make up for the deadbeat dads, we have paid young women to have children in sin. We have paid them *not* to get married. We have paid them to keep the father out of the home.

Rejecting family life. Jesus said, "He who has seen Me has seen the Father." [145] He was blessed to be part of a family. He knew that He looked like His Father, and that was a good thing to Him. He wanted to please His father. He is a model for us.

---

[143] Hebrews 12:8 KJV.
[144] Hebrews 12:9.
[145] John 14:9.

Some people struggle because they don't fit into a family, but maybe they don't want to be part of a family enough to accept the responsibility. They are not grown up enough to practice accountability and sharing. They want to be their own one-person family where no one can tell them when they're wrong. They need to join a church family and come to maturity so that God can use them.

> *When you become part of a family,*
> *you lose certain rights. You no longer represent*
> *yourself. Sons represent their father.*
> *That's part of the process.*
> *When you meet other people, they see the*
> *spirit of the father in the sons.*

The opposite is also true. When you are fatherless, it shows. Like the kids in the inner city. You can tell when those kids don't have a daddy, just as if they were carrying a signpost.

When you see fatherless church people, they look different, too. They are always jumping, never able to completely join in, always struggling. They are not willing to give up to become part of the family and come under a dad. They won't take the risk to make a move toward committed family life.

Running away from spiritual churches. Growing in God is a process that takes place best when you put down roots. People who are always jumping from church to church never establish roots that can nurture them while they grow. When they go jumping around, they're not looking for a stronger church. They're not looking for a greater miracle service or a higher spiritual level. They don't go where people are praying more, serving more, or giving more. They go to a lesser church, and they look for less involvement and less responsibility.

About ten years ago, to my amazement God showed up at Rock City Church and revival broke out. It was a genuine move of God. God was in the house. Yet even with us coming under a cloud of glory at every service, people actually left the church. I only use this as a reference. At that time, there were only three places in North America that were giving out that kind of evidence of revival: Brownsville, Toronto, and Baltimore. That doesn't mean that we had a corner on something, but I do believe that if God saw fit to show up and He spread the word about what was happening even though we had never advertised it, I would not expect people to leave rather than establish a lasting relationship.

They were not running to find God. They were running away from their responsibility to be changed in an environment of commitment.

Disrespect for God. The Bible assumes that people will respect their fathers, and if we respect them, how much more should we respect God? When people disrespect fathers, whom the Bible says are doing their best to help their sons, they are breaking one of the commandments, and also disrespecting God.

Subjection to God and our fathers brings life	*"Furthermore, we have had human fathers who corrected us, and we paid them respect. Shall we not much more readily be in subjection to the Father of spirits and live? For they indeed for a few days chastened us as seemed best to them, but He for our profit, that we may be partakers of His holiness."* [146]

Disrespect for pastors. You wouldn't expect someone to walk up to a preacher and say, "I don't like what you preach," but that's what people do today. They have lost respect for the office.

How would it look for me to walk up to your house to deliver a pizza and say, "I've got your pizza, but man, you

---

[146] Hebrews 12:9-10.

need to lose about 25 pounds. You're fat." You would tell me to take that pizza and wear it.

We've lost respect. We think we can walk into the house of God and say anything. We don't fear God and we don't respect the men of God He has put in place.

So what if fathers aren't always right. It doesn't matter. You're not in a position to correct your father. You're going to honor your father and mother, as the Bible says, and then you will be on your way to becoming a father yourself, someone whom others can honor. Of course I am not talking about the renegade pastors who bring shame to the name of God and the Church of Jesus Christ.

> *Most of the pastors you will meet are trying the best they know how to serve God and help you become all that you can by being a father to you. If they are out of order to an extreme level, that is a matter for their spiritual fathers and elders in the church and the city to correct.*

Telling your father what to say. I meet people all the time who are rebels wanting to debate the topic of my message. They think they should tell me what to say. Now I have no problem being challenged, but these people not only have no idea what they are talking about, but they also have no idea how to respect anyone. They don't fear God, and that is demonstrated in their irreverence for men of God. One individual had such an argumentative spirit it didn't matter what I preached, that person wanted to argue about it. Some people would argue with themselves. That's all they like to do. Just argue. They should be on one of those talk shows.

Telling your father what to do. Some people act like Elisha trying to tell Elijah what to do. It never works. After a period of time, they leave. What a shame. Instead of criticizing your spiritual father, stay connected. Give him some respect. He probably knows a lot more than you do.

I'm part of a family. I have a father. I have a spiritual

covering—a spiritual father in my life. I want to stay that way. Fathers aren't perfect. Elisha still had things to work on when Elijah left, but he was ready to lead as a father to others.

Youth ministries that produce rebels. The Church has opened the door to some problems with youth and I don't know if we can close it in time. We've got a generation of rebels. We will regret the day we opened the door to youth ministries that are nothing but music and entertainment, and don't teach youth how to respect their fathers, take chastening, and grow up to become spiritual fathers themselves.

Preference for brothers instead of fathers. In the church today, we don't want fathers. We want brothers. We want somebody to always agree with us or talk to us on our level. Fathers won't always agree with you. You can't brush them off. They will give you the rod of correction, if necessary, until you get your life straight.

Discipline is a sign of love	*"He who spares his rod hates his son, But he who loves him disciplines him promptly."* [147]

Somebody came to tell me about meeting with a father he hadn't seen for years. I told him it was a good thing to go and meet with his father.

We're relearning the importance of fathers. We're learning about fatherhood. We're learning about being sons and relating to fathers according to biblical order. Fathers aren't perfect, but fathers are fathers. We need them.

Feminizing the Gospel. We have brought into the church a feminized Gospel, but like it or not, the biblical Gospel is a masculine Gospel. Give me one reference where an angel was referred to as a woman. You think I'm treading on dangerous water there? Are you going to hold your tithe

---

[147] Proverbs 13:24.

and not come back to church any more? I just want you to agree that we need more men being men.

Carrying weights. We all carry a lot of extra weights. Doubt weighs us down. Finances are a weight. Children can be a weight. Marriage problems can be weights. The security of our nation can even be a weight. Fear, confusion, a religious spirit of condemnation, lust, addictions, pride and ego are weights. Guilt can become a 100-pound gorilla around your neck. Don't carry weights. Don't carry spirits of condemnation and failure.

People carry weights because of what they did or didn't do. That's what the Gospel is all about. Confess your sins, repent, get cleansed by the blood of Jesus, start a new life. If you get rid of those weights, you can run a better race to sonship.

If you are carrying that stuff, maybe you have carried it for years. When you got saved, you laid it down, but when you walked away from the altar, you reached back and grabbed that thing by the foot and have been carrying it around ever since. You're dragging a dead corpse around so that if this new life thing doesn't work out, you can always go back to that. You need to be free from that old dead weight. Jesus said, "Therefore if the Son makes you free, you shall be free indeed." [148] He came to give you life and life more abundantly. [149] You're free!

Lay aside the weights and run	". . . let us lay aside every weight, and the sin which doth so easily beset us, and let us run with patience the race that is set before us." [150]

Covering up. We all have weights that hinder us, but our attempts to cover them up make the burdens heavier. Some people carry the weight of sin because they know that

---

[148] John 8:36.
[149] See John 10:10.
[150] Hebrews 12:1 KJV.

they are living a lie. Maybe they are living in a sinful relationship. They cannot look you in the eye because of the weight of that thing. They need to strip off those things. Take off the layers and get real.

One night my wife and I watched an interview on TV. We could see that the woman being interviewed was not comfortable with who she was. She had weights. You could tell that she was covering up. Those weights made her uncomfortable in her own skin. Hidden weights will keep you from reaching your potential.

RESCUING THE SPIRITUAL ORPHANS

When the obstacles to sonship seem too great, some people who attend church as independents reject the church as their spiritual family, and therefore condemn themselves to the life of a spiritual orphan. Orphans have no family to represent. They only represent themselves. You will never have a true sense of purpose and belonging when you only represent yourself. Your vision will always be too small, because you are too small. You will not reproduce spiritual sons. You can't reproduce something that you don't have.

These spiritual orphans overcompensate for what they would normally receive from a father in the areas of protection and promotion. A father knows when to hold you back, and when to push you out there a little more. A self-promoting person will always push aggressively for his own way. Sometimes you won't see it, because they will be good at hiding it, but inside they are their own Number One.

Spiritual orphans seek churches with distant relationships, and keep their gifts trapped inside. They are self-protecting. They insulate themselves from penetrating remarks, no matter how harmless or helpful.

In a normal family, when it's time to eat dinner, even if you have been fussing with your brother and sister, you run down and eat together. You may have to get in bed that night next to the person who ticked you off.

104

Spiritual orphans don't understand family disagreements and that sort of thing, so they leave the first or second time they get offended because they don't understand what is happening. When they get offended, and they always do, they leave home and run away.

Spiritual orphans think they're in real danger if they stay, but like the teenage runaway, the real danger lurks outside the house. It's much better to stay in the family and get over it.

SUBMITTING TO FIND GOD'S MISSION

How do you run past all of the obstacles to sonship and break the curse of spiritual independence? You submit to your father and the vision of God for your life. What is submission? It is coming under the "mission" of God.

I'm blessed every time I see God break the hard shell of an "independent" soul. It's beautiful to see the inward treasures released when they finally trust and submit.

Your gifts are released through right connections to people. When you become a son, it's obvious to everybody that you have a daddy. People walk up to you and ask you where you go to church. They can tell you are part of something bigger than yourself.

Have you taken steps toward removing these obstacles to sonship in your own life and ministry? Can you see yourself as a son? Can you see yourself as a father? Because that is the next step in progression.

You will always be somebody's son, but when you come of age you will see yourself as a father and you will begin to inspire in others the same commitment to you that you have shown to your father.

the next chapter I want to give you a vision for the
ion of spiritual fathers so that the Church can
‿‿‿‿‿‿ a powerful, permanent force in the restoration and
reformation of society, but first I want you to join me in a
prayer.

Prayer to break an independent spirit

*"Father, I need Your help to break that independent spirit that
sits inside of me. I repent for it. I commit to You that I will
change my life from now on by my actions and by my words. I
don't want to be independent any longer. I don't want to be
thinking about myself all the time. I don't want to keep
protecting myself, serving myself, and promoting myself. I
want to submit myself to You and to those You have placed in
authority over me. I want to yield myself. I want to be part of a
family. Break this out of my life before it's too late, before I'm
unprofitable, before I rise up and choose my own will and end
up shipwrecked. Thank You, Father, that You have heard my
prayer. It's done. In Jesus' name I pray. Amen."*

CHAPTER 8

THE MAKING OF A GODLY FATHER

"Now, therefore, you are no longer strangers and foreigners, but fellow citizens with the saints and members of the household of God, having been built on the foundation of the apostles and prophets, Jesus Christ Himself being the chief cornerstone." [151]

I still remember the first funeral I attended with my pastor more than 30 years ago. He was trying to mentor me. We were sitting in a Baptist church. Red chairs, red pews, and red carpet. There we were, my pastor and I, sitting in two chairs with giant backs and big arms, right in front of everyone.

A few minutes went by. The deceased was lying in an open casket at the front of the church. A group of people got up and went over to the box. They started screaming and crying. I thought, *My God, I'm sad. This is a bummer for this family.* I'm thinking compassion.

All of a sudden, they took that casket and ran down the aisle with it! They were yelling. Somebody was hanging half off the side of the box as they were running down the aisle with that thing on wheels. I leaned over and said to my pastor, "Do you know where I can find the back door?" I'm thinking

---

[151] Ephesians 2:19-20.

about making a quick exit. My pastor didn't laugh; he was holding it real well.

He said later, "You almost made me lose it, boy." I didn't want to be there. What were they going to do next? They brought the box back. Later, I found out that they were professional hired mourners. Nobody liked the guy enough to cry, so they went and hired some people to do it for them.

When you die, will they have to go out on the streets saying, "I've got $20 here. Will you come in and cry?"

Say this with me: *"O God, let me make a difference. I don't want to have fake flowers and paid weepers when I die."*

LIVING TO PLEASE YOUR FATHER

The best way to become a godly father whom people respect when he dies is by being a godly son. Godly fathers are not born. They are made. They start out being sons who please their father.

God created us to want a father's love. When a young man makes a winning touchdown or dunks the basketball to win a game, he's not looking around for the approval of his fellow players. He's looking for his father's approval. God knew that if we didn't look for a father's approval, we wouldn't look for His approval. We wouldn't want God to be active in our lives.

When you have been loved and appreciated as a son, you can become a spiritual father who loves and appreciates other people.
You know how to forget about yourself and carry others through the hard times because your father has carried you.

When you become a spiritual father, you're the dad sitting in the stands cheering. You're the one giving your son some pointers on how to play a better game.

When spiritual fathers are missing, the children of the

generation become rebels. How can a rebel build the family name and make the name of the Lord great? He can't. Fathers take you past focusing on yourself and looking for someone to affirm you. They help you move beyond trying to get healed from past wounds.

When you become a father, you focus on fathering your children so that they can grow up and become great.

As a father, you know you can restore the children of this generation and help them overcome their rebellion, while lifting up the name of Jesus.

Keeping it real

Sometimes I talk to people at the end of a service and they are off in space somewhere. After I finish preaching, they come down and tell me something that doesn't even compute. It doesn't make sense. They're floating around so much you want to get a sandbag and tie it around their ankle to make them come down to earth.

People who have a godly father don't try to get away with flakiness like that. Their father and their family life have taught them how to keep it real.

When you're in a family and all you've got is one hotdog, and that hotdog hits the dinner table, and you've got eight kids plus Mom and Dad, you better have a foot-long hotdog because you're not going to get much otherwise. If someone is having his little pity party over in the corner and Mom says, "Time to eat," and he says, "I'm mad," they are going to say, "Oh, glory! I get more than an inch of hot dog. I might even get some relish this time."

Those sisters and brothers are not interested in your pout. They're saying, "If he's not coming to the table tonight, can we have his piece of hotdog?" You aren't even missed. What does the family want you to do? Grow up and get over it. Get back to the table.

⸢ELPING YOUR FATHER FIRST

h independent spirits run away from home and
⸝ ᴊᴜᴄᴇᴛs. They become prostitutes and sell their little
bodies to make money. They get in a gang so they can
identify. The next thing you know, they are part of the system
with a tag on their toe in a big black bag lying in the morgue.
Nobody cares because nobody knows. They were independent.

Why would you join a gang that does nothing but kill
people? Because you're looking for a family, but you want to
be independent from your parents. How do you break an
independent spirit? Join a real family and submit. Connect to
somebody else's vision and mission. You'll have a chance to
fulfill your own vision and mission later. Help your father
first. That's one of the ways you grow up so that God can give
you your own ministry when you're ready.

Faithful first with another man's vision	*"And if you have not been faithful in what is another man's, who will give you what is your own?"* [152]

My wife can tell you how many times I started out in
ministry and ended up quitting. Then I submitted and I became
an honorable son in the house of my father. I became a son
who never approached the pulpit without honoring my
spiritual father. I became a son and then God let me produce
sons.

MORE TIME TO WIN SOULS

Do you know how much time fathers in the church
have wasted in the last 20 years? We have had to spend every
day of church life correcting people who should be sons but
they won't listen. They won't submit. They keep doing the
same things wrong. They should be grown enough to know the

---

[152] Luke 16:12.

difference between right and wrong, but their pastors have to stop and spank them all the time. The leaders can't take the church to new levels. They're too busy dealing with the misbehaving babies.

God keeps blessing our church in Baltimore with resources to help the poor. Somebody gave us a whole thrift store. We got five tractor-trailer loads of milk and 40,000 pounds of potatoes. When we get opportunities like that to bless people and touch their lives and lead them to Christ, what do we have to do? We have to take time out from witnessing and winning souls to go deal with Sister Jelly Bean and Sister Butterbean who can't get along. Instead of growing up and coming of age, they still want milk. They keep saying, "I want you to bless me! I'm going to live like a rebel and do what I want to do, but bless me!"

If I could take all the pastors in our church and let them spend 20 percent of their time chasing unsaved people in the same way that they have had to chase already-saved people who want attention, this church couldn't hold the people we could bring in.

If I could tell the pastors, "You don't have to baby-sit and take care of people's little pouting fits any more. I want you to go and win souls every day," we'd have revival.

What has church life turned into? A couch and a bunch of crying towels. You join the church so that you can cry and tell them your problems instead of coming under accountability and getting with the program.

I could have a talk like this with everyone who is causing disruptions.

"Do you read the Bible?"

"No."

"Do you do what it says?"

"No."

"Do you intend to?"

"No."

"Have you ever done what anybody said?"

"No. Why are you asking?"

"Just thought I'd bring it up."

know how many preachers go home on Sunday that tomorrow won't come, because they know ...ave to do? They have just had a glorious ...y, out they know that on Monday they've got to answer phone calls about the message they preached to people who decided before they came in that they weren't going to listen to it. They weren't going to do what they heard.

Another prayer to break an independent spirit

"God, break that independent spirit in me. Let me come and be a part of a family. When it's not all perfect, help me to realize it's just a family. If I submit, I'm going to gain. If I don't, I'm going to lose. If I submit, I'm going to become part of a real family. I don't want to run any more. I don't want to go around offended all the time. I don't always want to have my point heard. I'll find a home and be a son of my father. In Jesus' name. Amen."

OUTPOURING FOLLOWS ORDER

God showed us the importance of order to an outpouring of the Holy Spirit when the apostles, waiting in the Upper Room, took time to add another man to replace Judas.

Taking time to establish godly government in the Church

"And they proposed two: Joseph called Barsabas, who was surnamed Justus, and Matthias. And they prayed and said, 'You, O Lord, who know the hearts of all, show which of these two You have chosen to take part in this ministry and apostleship from which Judas by transgression fell, that he might go to his own place.' And they cast their lots, and the lot fell on Matthias. And he was numbered with the eleven apostles." [153]

---

[153] Acts 1:23-26.

The number 12 in the numerology of the Bible is the number for government. Judas, the betrayer, was dead. Only 11 apostles were left. The number of apostles was incomplete. They needed 12. Numbers mean something in the Bible. We don't build doctrine around them, but they are important. Since the number 12 is the number of government, adding one more apostle would restore the number of apostles to 12, a biblical government.

God does things for a purpose. When He puts His emphasis on something, we need to pay attention and see what He's up to. The Bible emphasized the election of apostles after the resurrection of Jesus; therefore, it was significant. Once the government of 12 apostles was established, a major event happened—Pentecost, the great outpouring of the Holy Spirit. Was that just coincidental, or does it indicate that a divine purpose was being fulfilled when the apostles added a twelfth member, and then came the outpouring?

FOUNDATION OF APOSTLES AND PROPHETS

Apostles are significant in biblical government. The Bible says that the Church is built on the foundation of apostles and prophets.

Built on the foundation of the apostles and prophets, Jesus Christ Himself being the Chief Cornerstone

"Now, therefore, you are no longer strangers and foreigners, but fellow citizens with the saints and members of the household of God, having been built on the foundation of the apostles and prophets, Jesus Christ Himself being the chief cornerstone, in whom the whole building, being fitted together, grows into a holy temple in the Lord, in whom you also are being built together for a dwelling place of God in the Spirit." [154]

---

[154] Ephesians 2:19-22.

When the foundation is destroyed, the righteous don't know what to do. They lack direction without that authoritative voice of apostles and prophets who are fathers in the land.

Confusion with no foundations	*"If the foundations are destroyed, What can the righteous do?"* [155]

However, it is also true that when the foundations are in place, the righteous do know what to do. As God restores His governmental structure, they get their hearts right toward authority and align themselves under His order in the Church.

Pentecost followed restored government

After the apostles went through that administrative process and chose the twelfth apostle, Pentecost followed. I don't have any way of knowing for sure, but that leads me to believe that before there is an outpouring of God, there has to be a government in place to deal with the impact of the outpouring. It tells me that because a governmental order was in place before God's glory came, there was a divine vehicle for that glory to rest upon. God did not pour out His spirit onto a disorderly Church. They had brought themselves under His order. Outpouring followed the establishment of that order.

So many times churches wonder, "Why isn't God pouring out His Spirit on my church?" Often, it's because people are out of order. Their lives are like yo-yos, up and down, up and down. They bounce all over. They don't have a location. They don't have a home. They don't submit to anybody. They're just a bunch of hippies.

When you neglect God's order, you have fleshly chaos. That is true on a corporate level in the church, on an individual level, and in the home. When you neglect God's order in your own life, your marriage, and your family, you have chaos. God's spirit is hindered by that mess.

When churches come in line with the order of the

---

[155] Psalm 11:3.

apostles and prophets and everything else related to c structure, we might be at Chapter One of the next gre outpouring, and Chapter Two is about to happen. I believe we're on the edge of something. I believe that Jesus has saved the best wine for last.[156] If we cooperate with Him in the reestablishment of God's government and order in the earth, we will get that wine.

As God is restoring the foundation of the apostles and prophets to the Church, books are being written by apostles. Conferences are bringing together apostles from Africa and other nations. Apostles are meeting in Jerusalem. That tells me that something is about to bring the Church back to divine order.

In times of war, generals come and reason together. They strategize together, and they always have a purpose. They plan new campaigns. Is God placing an emphasis here that we need to see?

Your willingness to get yourself in order is vital to this next outpouring. If you refuse to align yourself with God, He will accomplish His sovereign will without you.

Prayer to come under government
"Lord, send a Holy Ghost revival. Make me a son [daughter]. Since You're getting your government in order, teach me how I can get my life in order. If my life is out of order, the government will have no army to raise up, but if I get my life in order, then You can do something awesome through me as part of an army reaching others. In Jesus' name."

LOVE IN THE CHURCH HONORS THE FATHER

When the churches get united, we will become an army. The pastors in Baltimore should be an army with each division under the government of God, but they are divided

---

[156] John 2:10.

and fragmented. We have a group of pastors whom we have brought together, but it's been a labor. I heard Pat Robertson say, "I'm amazed. Most people have not survived Baltimore." Billy Sunday referred to it as "the graveyard of preachers." I ate dinner with Oral Roberts and he said, "Can any good thing come out of this city? I have heard a good report, my brother. You have accomplished something for God." We're rejoicing because we have 80 to 100 pastors somewhat working together, but there are 1600 churches in this area.

The same business of envy, jealousy, and division that goes on in the city goes on in the local church. One person won't work for this one. Another won't serve that one. They don't want to do this and that.

Sons spread love

It is God's will for us to love one another as sons of one Father. We are to love one another as Jesus has loved us.

| Commandment to love as Jesus loves | "A new commandment I give to you, that you love one another; as I have loved you, that you also love one another. By this all will know that you are My disciples, if you have love for one another." [157] |

It's a sad day when people in the Body of Christ deal with one another as if they were serving different gods.

| Unity because we have one father and one God | "Have we not all one Father? Has not one God created us? Why do we deal treacherously with one another By profaning the covenant of the fathers?" [158] |

---

[157] John 13:34-35.
[158] Malachi 2:10.

116

When we have wrong attitudes toward one another, God takes it seriously. The Bible says it comes down to profaning the covenant of the fathers. When we do those things, we embarrass our fathers. Our fathers get a bad name.

The body of Christ can't build a reputation for jealousy and strife. We must build father and son relationships according to the model of Jesus and His Father. Mature sons don't let envy, jealousy, and division come between them, because that profanes the name of the Father. Only ungodly sons deal treacherously with one another. Sons spread love.

Some people spread rumors about things that don't even exist about their pastors and leaders. They create turmoil within a city so that preachers don't like each other because they heard something from some sheep. I've always said that wolves come in sheep's clothing. We can do better than that.

Doing something God-like, like your father

When you get close to something God is doing through your father, and your life has come into biblical order, you may start doing something God-like, as your father did. You might be stuck at the Jordan and everybody is waiting and saying, "Let's see if he's got it." You have an old coat in your hand that belonged to an old prophet. You roll it up; you smack the water and you say, "Let the God of Elijah show up now!" [159] All of a sudden, the water opens up and you say, "Good God! It is with me!" Watch the story of Elisha's life. When he leaves Elijah he starts doing miracles like you can't believe because he has a double portion. He's got Elijah's anointing and his too.

Remember, the students in the school of the prophets didn't relate to Elijah as sons, but Elisha was a son who said, "I am going to stay and watch you. I am going to watch where you are, I am going to watch what you do, and I am going to stay close enough to see what is going on around you." When you stop being a student and you start moving into wanting that Elisha spirit of a son, you are not trying to rush out of

---

[159] See 2 Kings 2.

church as soon as the service is over. You are not trying to get away from the pastor and what God is doing through him. You are looking for what you can do to serve him without being told so you can get right up close.

When you serve an apostle or prophet, you are watching the man of God and the things that God is doing through him at a level that influences the generation. You are seeing what God is up to. You are a watchman.

Some people in the church are like the students, and some have the passion of Elisha who wanted something from God through his father. If you are like the students, you just come to church to get a bunch of knowledge and hang around somebody who says, "Praise the Lord, Amen." You tell a story that is not even your testimony. You're not the real thing. You're not even close to being like God. When you decide that you want to be a son, you will change your whole lifestyle for the sake of being like Jesus.

Sonship is vital to your future. Your relationship with your father—spiritual and natural—is essential for you to be a part of the next Book of Acts.

I wonder if my father . . .
When I was growing up as a Christian, I never had a day where I said, "I wonder if my Pastor . . ." I didn't go there. I went to my prayer room and built a strong prayer life so I didn't have to go around with a spirit of suspicion. I had a spirit of discernment. I didn't have to say, "I wonder if my pastor's motives are wrong. He is going to make a mistake. He is human, so he is going to . . ." I just went and prayed. I said, *"Father, You love me. If I ask for bread, You will not give me a stone. So God, I thank You, even if my pastor is a jackass, let him prophesy,* [160] *then afterwards let him stay a jackass because all I want is what You want."* I said, *"God talk to me, and I mean talk to me clearly!"* Then I said, *"Lord, use him because that is the right way."*

My pastor never, ever made a mistake in my life

---

[160] See Numbers 22.

118

because I didn't let him.

I make mistakes all the time. I come in my ˌ
tell all of it. I tell everything I do. Sometimes my wife can ˌ
believe it. She'll even say, "Don't tell it all," but I'd rather be
real and be full of God.

When we empty ourselves of the weights of pride and
selfishness, then we can be filled with the power to overcome
death, hell, and the grave. At the last supper, Jesus got naked
and He conquered everything, but when you put on, you can't
conquer anything. Every weight has to be cast off. We have to
follow His example with our lives. Usually in our most
pressing moments and our greatest hour of testing, we put on
rather than take off. Jesus was running out of time so He
stripped down. Maybe we're running out of time. It's the end
of the supper and just hanging out and fellowshipping with
Jesus isn't enough. We have to make ourselves ready for the
final hour.

CONFUSION ABOUT MARRIAGE

We have a fatherless generation, a prayerless
generation, and a wicked generation. Who would have
believed we would actually be living in a day when we had to
defend marriage? The onslaught against marriage is a natural
sequence of events because the Church has failed to provide
leadership for the family. We have the power to reverse this
decline, but it won't reverse itself. We have to make some
aggressive moves, or it will get worse.

When you take out the mainstay of a family—the
father—it opens the door to massive confusion about what
marriage and the family look like. Marriage was not at fault
and marriage was not the problem. The problem was that
fathers were pulled out of marriage and then we said, "What is
marriage?"

Since the Garden of Eden, Lucifer has been coming
along and saying those little things, "Did God say. . .?" That's
what's going on today. I look at it and I say, "Wow!"

Fatherlessness has even brought our Constitution under attack to the place where we need an amendment to define marriage as the union of a man and a woman. It came about because fathers became absent.

That's what happened in the natural. However, we remember that we are never just talking about what is happening with natural fathers and their children. We know about the realm of the Spirit. The Bible says that many times the natural comes first,[161] but it models or shows us the spiritual condition at the root.

When we see natural decline, like what is happening in the state of marriage, we can look over in the spiritual and see a decline there, too. That shifts our focus to where it belongs—the Church.

I'M COVERED EVERY DAY

The understanding of sonship could change your life. It could bring you into a place of accountability and power.

As I told you, I have somebody who covers my life and my wife's life, and he speaks into our lives. Whether I was a preacher or not, I wouldn't spend a day without a covering. I wouldn't spend a day when I didn't have my heart right with my pastor. I can talk to Pastor Charles Green. He calls my house all the time. He writes me letters all the time. When I say all the time, I mean all the time. He can tell me, "Son, don't do this. Don't do that. You better pray about this."

Pastor Green called me one day when I was getting on a plane. He said, "God told me to tell you not to get on that plane." I didn't get on the plane. That's somebody who loves me. I gave him permission to do that for the sake of the greatness of God coming forth from my life.

---

[161] See 1 Corinthians 15:46.

Prayer of repentance

"Father, may I learn to use words like 'I submit, I
have a covering, I have a Father.' May I use those
be glad. May I say that I'm going to make Your name great on
the earth because I'm going to be a son of honor, a son who
makes Your name worthy. I can only ask You to use me, Lord,
to somehow reveal what You're trying to say.

I know, Lord, You're trying to speak to the body of
Christ. You're trying to speak to individuals and trying to
speak collectively. May I do what I must do to bring my life in
line for the Great Day, Father. May I examine myself and say
that maybe I've been one of those people who did what I
wanted to do when I wanted to do it. Lord, help me. Forgive
me, Lord. I'm going to try to bring myself to a place to submit.
I have not done it well, but I want to change. I need
submission. I'm making the name of God a reproach by my
rebellion. Forgive me, Lord. Help me to change. In Jesus'
name. Amen."

Is that your prayer? Ask God to show you those areas where
you need to repent, then repent, and then say this prayer.

Prayer for making God's name great

"Lord, make me a son who will bring honor to Your name.
May Your name never be brought down in the drudgery of
humanity's sin and selfishness. May Your name always be like
a banner high above everything. Today, Lord, make me a son
[daughter], who is pleasing to You. In Jesus' name. Amen."

Repentance and getting ourselves in order are
necessary because we have something of great importance that
we are about to undertake. We are preparing ourselves to
become that miracle generation that fulfills the will of God in
earth as it is in heaven. Through our obedience, God will
change the earth.

Do you want to join that miracle generation today? Do
you want to know what God expects to accomplish through
people who are willing to do things His way, today, in every

area of their lives? Can you believe for a reversal in the decline that we have seen in recent years because of something that you do, even if no one else is willing to answer the call?

CHAPTER 9

THE MIRACLE GENERATION

And he said to him, "Every man at the beginning
sets out the good wine, and when the guests have
well drunk, then the inferior. You have kept the
good wine until now!" [162]

In November 1989, I was behind the Berlin Wall when a miracle happened. The wall was opened. Traffic flowed between the zones of that divided city. Families were reunited. Germany entered a new era. My passport was stamped when I went in past the barbed wire, but it was never stamped going out. The world had changed in a single day.

All of a sudden, we are at the wedding feast with Jesus[163] and His disciples, and the wine is good, but something is about to happen right before our eyes. Some new wine has been produced in secret that is about to be brought forth, and it will amaze even the master of the feast. The grapes for the new wine have been plucked, crushed, and stepped on. We are that new wine. God has crushed us like grapes. He has squeezed us and worked with us until we can produce the wine of the Spirit that is the best wine anyone has ever tasted.

---

[162] John 2:10.
[163] See John 2.

In my generation and the one before me, there has been good wine. There has been good preaching, and we have had our revival meetings. Christian television has increased. We have Promise Keepers. We have The Call. God has done some good things with the wine that we have had.

Everybody at the feast has been drinking this pretty good wine, but a miracle is about to take place. There is new wine at the wedding. The wine taster is ready to taste the best wine he's ever had—the pure virgin stuff. A miracle generation is being birthed.

This miracle generation will birth the most radical church you have ever seen. The arts will be exploding. New songs of the Lord will be heard. The Church will taste the best anointing it has ever tasted, the best outpouring, the best revival, the best move of God, the best music, and the best arts.

The Church will bring kids back from the failures of past youth ministries to the place where they worship God and they live righteous and holy lives. We will find the people who just got out of the way, but they have gifts. They will come back into the Church, and God will use them. A young man came to Rock City Church right after he got out of jail. He told his mom that the first place he wanted to go was back to church. Why did he have to go to jail? He said to me, "I just got out of the way."

God can use people in the midst of any circumstances if they want to be doers of the Gospel and not just hearers.[164] I have seen people, right in the middle of a move of God, who just wanted to go to church and attend conferences to hear new speakers. They wanted new TV programs and new churches, but they didn't want God's mantle. If you don't have His mantle, all you have is a little knowledge to plug into your new thing, but if you have His mantle, when it comes time to cross the Jordan, you can smack the river and it opens up.

A day is coming when speakers will not be invited back when nothing miraculous happens while they are there.

---

[164] See James 1:22.

The ones invited back will be those who make something happen. God has anointed them for action.

THE BEST WINE COMES LAST

The wedding feast is coming to an end, but before it does, something is about to change. While we have been drinking the wine of my generation, another outpouring of God is on the horizon and it's going to be like nothing that we have tasted before.

When Jesus was at the wedding in Cana,[165] some good wine was being served. Everybody was happy with it, but the wine ran out. Nobody said, "The wine is bad, give us better." The wine just ran out. The generation that we have been drinking from has been good wine of the Spirit, but it is running out. It's not time to throw the wine away, but the wine is coming to an end and it's miracle time.

Some pitchers are sitting around at the wedding. They are empty and available. There are six of them, which is the number of man, and Jesus is about ready to blow the thing wide open. He is saying, "Fill them up with water!" [166]

The water will be sitting there, and all of a sudden Jesus will transform the water into the greatest wine ever tasted by the Church. Everyone who wants it will be drinking new wine that's pure and fresh and more potent than any wine they have ever had before.

Do you want something from God? Do you want to partake of the new wine or do you want to be stuck with what you have been drinking? A miracle is ready to happen right in front of you. Right in the middle of the church there is a miracle. There is a colorless group sitting right in the church. Colorless! But a miracle is about ready to take place. It's time to get some water pots because the best is coming on the scene. The water is about ready to be turned into a miracle.

---

[165] See John 2.
[166] See John 2:7.

I am going to be at this wedding. Our wine is running out. I'm going to flavor those young bucks. I'll be one of those who makes sure they get home after they drink. I'll be their designated driver. I am going to drive this new group where they're going because I want to be in the middle of what God is doing next.

Some people don't even know if God has ever showed up or not. They have let themselves become cold, indifferent, and casual. They don't even think about Christ and prayer. God is about ready to cause a miracle to happen and they are going to miss it, while the Elishas are saying, "I want the mantle. I want what God has!"

Compared to what little we have seen happen here in the United States in the past 20 years, what is happening in the mission field should shame us. The fastest growing churches in the world are not in America but in other nations: churches 6 years old with 80,000 people; 9 years old with 55,000 people. We need some new wine. We need to be finished with the old ideas and old theologies and fears that have gripped us and kept us paralyzed, and prevented us from embracing the new thing that God wants to do with His Church.

This thing that is happening around the world is a fresh move of God. I talked to an overseas pastor who said, "Our Muslim president is praying with me on a regular basis now." That will shake the nation when he wins that president to Christ and he changes his whole connection with Islam. Islam is collapsing. It is falling apart. Nations right now—leaders, presidents, and heads of nations—are being put in the hands of godly men and women. They have it in their eyes; they are the next Elishas coming on the scene.

I know of a place in Algeria where they had a meeting with God. People were praying and a whole village had a revelation of Jesus Christ and every one of them turned from their Muslim faith. It was during Ramadan. There are 20 million Christians praying for those Arabs to have a meeting with Jehovah God and not Allah. If we think that we can change this issue by hiding in the church saying, "Praise the Lord," we're mistaken. We need to get out there and do something. We need some new wine.

The wine taster said, "How is it that you have saved the best for the last?" [167] We are at the end of this wedding, not the beginning. The best is about to come. What I have seen happening in missions gives me hope that we are at the great day where this miracle of transformation is about to happen everywhere, including America.

THE MIRACLE GENERATION

The old generation went through crushings that the new one won't have to go through. They will go through their "necessaries," but God is going to make them a miracle generation. Their time of coming of age is shortened. The time of water changing to wine is shorter than grapes being made into wine. My generation has been grapes made into wine, but there is a generation right now that is going to be water made into wine. One day we are going to wake up and the wine is going to be served and we are not even going to know when it happened.

I met some young men who are pastoring three churches that are exploding. They are buying a big department store that closed down. I looked into one of the young pastor's eyes, and I saw something. Here was a young man who was not in this thing just to get some knowledge and look at things from a distance. This guy was after something. He wanted an impartation that would change the generation through him.

Elijah was a great man, and all the students around him wanted his mantle, but he chose Elisha, a businessman. Businessmen are going to start prospering. They will start being favored. People will start getting raises because they are so outstanding in their jobs.

I have it in my spirit. I am praying it. I am tasting it. I am walking in it. It is God in this day for His Church!

I believe that we'll have a revival that will eclipse all

---

[167] See John 2:10.

revivals we have ever known. It will make all the news broadcasts. It will make other news look like nothing.

Overcoming bad memories
Maybe you had a bad father. Face it today. Stop running from it. Stop hiding. Deal with it. You're mad. You're angry. You're hurt. You didn't have a good father. Don't let it drive you for the rest of your life so you have to be rejected by those whom God puts in your path to bring you to sonship. God puts sons in the path of fathers so that they can learn how to be sons. Regardless of his attitude toward you or his lack of willingness to reach out and reconcile with you, repent for your unforgiveness. If he's still alive, go and see him with forgiveness in your heart so you can move on.

Saying yes to Jesus
Jesus loves you. He has a purpose for you. You don't have to live your independent life serving your own self anymore. Today you can say yes to Jesus. I want to stop and pray for you right now.

"Father, I pray right now, if anyone has never said yes to You, may they say yes right now. May they bow their heart, and say yes to You."

Pray this prayer
"Today I want Jesus in my life. Today I want to submit to the Lord as never before."

Don't be ashamed. It's all right. It's the best prayer you ever prayed. I'll pray for you now: *"Father, bless them in Jesus' name. Reveal Yourself to them. Show them Your love. Show them Your mercy. Show them Your tender, loving mercy, Father, today. Oh, God, change their lives forever. What a good day, Lord."*

JOY IN THE JOURNEY

I have a final word for you to put in your heart. It's *"joy."* Hebrews 12:2 says that Jesus, "for the joy that was set before Him endured the cross, despising the shame, and has sat down at the right hand of the throne of God." [168]

Hebrews 12 starts like this:

"Therefore we also, since we are surrounded by so great a cloud of witnesses . . ." [169]

That cloud of witnesses means those who have gone before us—that great abundance of patriots who look out of the portholes of heaven to watch the world. They're already in the grandstands. David and Elijah, and Jeremiah, and all of them. A great cloud of witnesses watches us, to the glory of God.

Running with endurance because we have no extra weights | *". . . let us lay aside every weight, and the sin which so easily ensnares us, and let us run with endurance the race that is set before us, looking unto Jesus, the author and finisher of our faith."* [170]

Jesus is the Author of the Book, and Jesus finished the race to secure our victory. What was His focus as He ran? Joy.

". . . who for the joy that was set before Him endured the cross." [171]

There was joy in the journey that Jesus ran for us. I encourage you today to see that there can be joy in your journey if you keep your eyes on Jesus and look for joy His

---

[168] Hebrews 12:2.
[169] Hebrews 12:1.
[170] Hebrews 12:1-2.
[171] Hebrews 12:2.

way, the way of the cross.

> *. . . endured the cross, despising the shame, and has sat down at the right hand of the throne of God.*[172]

LEAVING ROOM FOR THE UNEXPECTED

Some people will criticize the new wine and fight the new moves because they don't want to change, and they don't have room in their lives for the unexpected any more. Jesus had to endure all of that and more, but He endured the cross, while despising the shame, and pressed on to sit down at the right hand of the throne of God.

Pray this prayer
"God, I am going to be part of this miracle generation. I am not going to sit back and become grumpy, dead, and half-baked and lose everything I have ever worked for. I hear what you are saying. I want to be part of the miracle generation. I want to be among those who can taste of the old wine and say with gratitude, 'Thank God for it,' but I am ready to drink of the new wine. In Jesus' name. Amen."

Lord, make us a miracle generation.

---

[172] Hebrews 12:2.

ABOUT THE AUTHOR

Bishop Bart Pierce serves as senior pastor of Rock City Church, 1607 Cromwell Bridge Road, Baltimore, Maryland 21234. Phone: 410-882-2217. Website: www.rockcitychurch.com. His wife of 36 years, Coralee, serves as pastoral assistant to her husband. The church is growing and vibrant, with a multi-racial expression. It has a unique calling to reach out to the lost and hurting with a vision of what God is doing today. Bishop Pierce is co-founder of Global Compassion Network, which includes organizations around the world such as Operation Blessing, Somebody Cares International, World Relief, Operation Compassion, and others. He also provides apostolic oversight to churches in the United States, Ukraine, Ghana, and Madagascar.

Ministries of Compassion that Bishop Pierce has pioneered include:

Adopt A Block: taking the city of Baltimore back block by block.
Can Can Make a Difference: feeding program for the impoverished that distributes a million pounds of food a year.
Nehemiah House: shelter for homeless men that has given a fresh start to more than 5,000 men formerly tormented by a life of drugs, alcohol and crime.
The Hiding Place: home for pregnant women and women in crisis situations.

Since January 1997, Rock City Church has experienced a mighty outpouring of God's presence. People have come from around the world to seek God's face. Many have experienced miraculous healings, deliverances, and a renewed relationship with the Lord. As a result, Bishop Pierce has formed numerous relationships with pastors and leaders. He has a passion for unity in the body of Christ. He is a member of the International Coalition of Apostles (ICA), the Apostolic Council of Prophetic Elders (founded by Dr. Peter Wagner and Cindy Jacobs), which includes members such as Jim Goll, Tommy Tenney, Beth Alves, Chuck Pierce, Dutch Sheets, and others. He also promotes unity in the city of Baltimore by fostering relationships with area pastors and their congregations, and serves as president of Peace For The City, a coalition of Baltimore metropolitan pastors. He has served on the executive board for The Call DC, a gathering of more than 300,000 youth in September 2000. He was the National Youth Coordinator for Washington For Jesus. He has appeared numerous times on CBN and has spoken in many churches and conferences throughout the world. The heart of his mission is to see the next generation run after God.

Other Books by Bishop Bart Pierce
Seeking Our Brothers: Restoring Compassionate Christianity to the Church
Publisher: Fresh Bread (August 20, 2000). ISBN: 0768421004.
Author shares his heart for the people that nobody wants.
Available online www.rockcitychurch.com bookstore.

Bishop Pierce Also Contributed Chapters to the Following:
Che Ahn, *Hosting the Holy Spirit.* Authored chapter entitled "Serving Humanity."
Publisher: Renew (November 1, 2000). ISBN: 0830725849

Tommy Tenney, *Mary's Prayers and Martha's Recipes*
Publisher: Fresh Bread (February 1, 2002). ISBN: 0768420598